MW01200159

Waist-Deep in Dung

Waist-Deep in Dung

A Stomach-Churning Look at the Grossest Jobs Throughout History

CHRISTINE VIRNIG

ILLUSTRATED BY KORWIN BRIGGS

GODWINBOOKS

HENRY HOLT AND COMPANY

NEW YORK

Henry Holt and Company, *Publishers since 1866*
Henry Holt® is a registered trademark of Macmillan Publishing Group, LLC
120 Broadway, New York, NY 10271 • mackids.com

Text copyright © 2024 by Christine Virnig
Illustrations copyright © 2024 by Korwin Briggs
All rights reserved.

Our books may be purchased in bulk for promotional, educational, or business
use. Please contact your local bookseller or the Macmillan Corporate and
Premium Sales Department at (800) 221-7945 ext. 5442 or by email at
MacmillanSpecialMarkets@macmillan.com.

Library of Congress Cataloging-in-Publication Data is available.

First edition, 2024
Book design by Liz Dresner and Julia Bianchi
Printed in the United States of America by BVG, Fairfield, Pennsylvania

ISBN 978-1-250-76235-1

1 3 5 7 9 10 8 6 4 2

This book is dedicated to my A-M-A-Z-I-N-G husband.
I would totally swim through a sewer for you!

TABLE OF CONTENTS

PART 1: THE GROSSEST JOBS DEALING WITH BLOOD, MEDICINE, AND DEAD BODIES

PART 2: THE GROSSEST JOBS DEALING WITH POOP, PEE, AND VOMIT

Waist-Deep in Dung

FOREWORD

AS YOU'VE PROBABLY guessed from the title of this book, you will soon be learning about a whole slew of really gross jobs. Jobs that deal with poop. Vomit. Blood-sucking leeches. Decomposing bodies.

And more than once, I'm sure you'll find yourself wondering why, why, why the workers didn't just quit. Why not find a nice, cozy, feces-free desk job instead?

Well, there are lots of possible reasons. For one, they may have stayed on the job because they *wanted* to. Everybody has different likes and dislikes. I don't mind dealing with blood, but the sight of maggots makes my stomach churn as though I've just swallowed a handful of, well, maggots. But my gets-faint-at-the-sight-of-a-paper-cut neighbor might think wriggling, squishy insect larvae are fascinating. To this I say, "Yay for our differences!" Because they mean my maggot-loving neighbor can deal with all the maggots. And I'll stick to blood.

Another reason people do yucky-sounding jobs is because they have to. It's like that time your sister went on a spicy food kick and wound up with diarrhea so foul it would make a hippo blush. And then your dad told YOU to clean the toilet! The whole thing was so colossally unfair that you wanted to refuse, but then it would be bye-bye video games for a month. So you pulled up your sleeves, plugged your nose, grabbed the toilet bowl brush, and got to work. You didn't *want* to do the job, but if you were ever going to play *Minecraft* again, you had no choice.

Plenty of people similarly do jobs they don't like, even jobs they hate, because they feel stuck. There might not be any other jobs out there for someone with their skill set, yet they still need money to buy food. Pay rent. Purchase medications. They simply can't afford to quit. Or—as is the case for a couple of the jobs in this book—they aren't *allowed* to quit.

And, finally, it's important to remember that many of the jobs found within these pages took place centuries or even millennia ago. Back when poop routinely filled waterways, overflowed cesspits, and sometimes even piled up in the streets. Back when doctors thought drilling a hole into someone's skull was a reasonable way to treat a headache. Back when there were no such things as robot vacuum cleaners or self-cleaning litter boxes or full-body hazmat suits, and everything had to be done by hand. In other words, back when the bulk of the population had no access to nice, cozy, feces-free desk jobs.

Bottom line: As we read about these jobs, as strange

and distasteful as they might seem, let's try not to judge the people who did them. Let's remember that some of the workers liked their jobs; others hated them. Some did a specific job by choice; others had no other option. And throughout it all, we are all a product of our time. Our place. And our culture.

A WARNING!

STOP READING FOR a second and picture your dream job. The job you can see yourself happily doing day after day, week after week, year after year, for your entire adult life.

Well? What job did you pick?

Were you a firefighter? An actor? An astronaut?

Maybe you chose a job full of fun and adventure. Or one that promises a big paycheck. Or maybe you dream of someday solving one of Earth's great mysteries. Like what came before the Big Bang? Why did T. rex have such tiny arms? And where do all your socks disappear to?

Whatever career you picked, odds are good that you did NOT pick any of the jobs you'll read about in this book. Unless you dream of jumping into sewers, digging up dead bodies, or stomping around in vats of stale pee, that is.

But even if your life's goal isn't to become the king's toilet paper holder, a professional leech collector, or a puke cleaner-upper, it can nonetheless be fascinating to learn about these jobs. Because by modern-day standards, they're gross. They're revolting. And yet people did them.

Before you keep reading, though, I do need to give a

A Warning

quick warning. This book is not for everyone. Not only are all the jobs disgusting in one way or another, but some of the chapters deal with pretty disturbing stuff. Like maggoty dead bodies and being buried alive. If this doesn't sound like your cup of tea, there's no shame in putting this book back on the shelf and grabbing something else.

But if you think your stomach can handle it, then go ahead.

Turn the page!

PART 1

THE GROSSEST JOBS DEALING WITH BLOOD, MEDICINE, AND DEAD BODIES

Chapter 1

Mummy Making

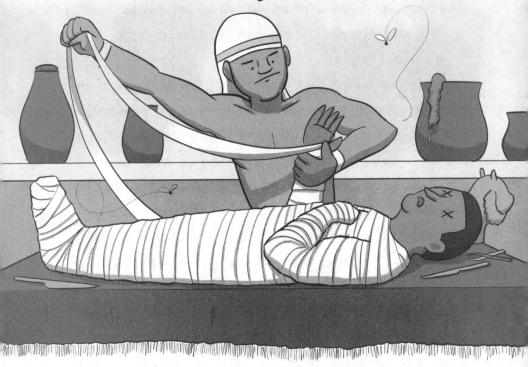

Job: Egyptian Embalmer
Time Period: Ancient Egypt

Mummy. What do you think of when you hear that word? Halloween? A scary movie? Or maybe those awesome mummy cupcakes your mom once made for your kindergarten class?

If you're like me, you sometimes get so wrapped up in the Hollywood version of a mummy that you forget what one truly is. That hidden under all those brown, three-thousand-year-old linens there is an *actual* body. The body of a person who once had parents, friends, and annoying siblings. A person who had thoughts and feelings. Fears and dreams.

A person like you.

When that person died, their grieving family handed their body over to an embalmer—the I-have-a-*really*-gross-job star of this chapter. But what exactly the embalmer did with the body varied significantly depending on when the person died. This is because ancient Egyptians were busy making mummies for about three *thousand* years. If you consider that the United States has been a country for less than three *hundred* years, it's obvious the ancient Egyptians were creating mummies for a very, very, *very* long time.

When first starting out, the embalmers were fairly clueless. They weren't sure how to preserve a body, so they didn't worry about that little detail. Instead they simply wrapped it up all pretty, tried to make everything look as lifelike as possible, and called it good.

Those early mummy makers definitely had a gruesome job; they had to handle dead bodies all day long. But at least they didn't need to deal with blood and guts. Never fear, though, the blood and guts were coming soon. Because those early mummies simply weren't up to snuff. Instead of staying preserved for year after year, they rotted away. Decomposed. And ultimately reeked worse than your brother's hockey jersey after a big game.

Enjoy Wailing? Make It Your Job!

When a person died in ancient Egypt, their family was left behind to grieve their loss. But if the family was wealthy enough, they wouldn't have to do all the grieving alone. They could hire professional mourners.

These mourners—who were typically women—went around wailing and sobbing over the death of a person they'd probably never met. They tore at their clothes, scratched their skin, threw dust on their heads. Their job was simple: make sure everyone knew that a rich, important person had died.

Amazingly, professional mourners didn't exist only in Egypt—they were found in multiple ancient cultures. Not only that, there are still people who make money by hiring themselves out as mourners at funerals today. Until it closed its doors in 2019, there was even a company in England called Rent-A-Mourner!

Why did this happen?

Because the bodies—left virtually untouched under the wrappings—were more than 50 percent water. And that water allowed organisms like bacteria and maggots to feed upon the corpses and break them down. So if the embalmers wanted their mummies to last, it was clear they needed to turn their attention to the bodies themselves. They needed to eliminate the pesky water that allowed the flesh-eating critters to do their whole flesh-eating thing.

Step one in Operation No More Water was to remove the organs. To get them out, a person called a slitter cut a several-inches-long incision in the corpse's abdomen. As soon as the cut was made, the slitter ran away.

Fast.

Because soon everyone in the vicinity would be chasing him, yelling at him, throwing rocks at him.

Why would they do this?

Because the slitter had done a horrific thing. He'd cut into a dead body. He'd violated a corpse. And this was a major no-no in ancient Egypt. Who cared that everyone at the time *wanted* to be mummified when they died and that the slitter performed a necessary part of the process? The slitter was chased nonetheless.

While the slitter was busy running away, the embalmer got to work on the now-cut-open body. He reached in and started yanking stuff out. He pulled out the liver. The stomach.

Why Make a Mummy?

You're probably wondering why the ancient Egyptians bothered with mummy making at all. Why not bury the bodies as is or cremate them and get on with it? The answer has everything to do with the afterlife.

The ancient Egyptian afterlife was the Place to Be after death, but getting there was anything but easy. Multiple obstacles stood in the way, like Ammit—the part-lion, part-hippopotamus, part-crocodile goddess who'd gobble up any human hearts that weren't deemed good enough.

Furthermore, to have any shot at making it into the afterlife and surviving there, a body needed to be reunited with parts of its spirit, called the *ka* and the *ba*. According to one popular theory on mummification, the *ka* and *ba* only reunited with a body *if they recognized it*. Which means if the body got all rotten or was missing a pinky toe or if it simply didn't look close enough to the person in question, the *ka* and *ba* might not be able to find it.

No *ka*. No *ba*.
No afterlife.

Hence the mummy!

Yard after yard of snakelike intestines. He broke through the diaphragm and removed the lungs. The heart he left in place; it was needed if a person wanted a shot at getting into the ancient Egyptian afterlife.

Mummy Medicine

I wish "Mummy Medicine" referred to the medicine your mum gives you when you have a headache. But, sadly, this isn't the case. It refers to actual ancient Egyptian mummies that were ground up and sold as medicine all across Europe.

The whole mummies-as-medicine thing started because of a huge misunderstanding. In the Middle East, *mumiya* or *mumia* was a naturally occurring bitumen (which is a black, tar-like substance) highly valued in medicine. Some say it was prized more than gold.

Well, apparently the dark, resinous material covering ancient Egyptian mummies looked an awful lot like *mumia*. So it was given the same name.

When Europeans started translating Arabic medical texts, whenever they saw *mumiya* or *mumia* listed, they unfortunately didn't think of the innocent bitumen version of *mumia*. Not at all.

They thought of mummy coverings.

This disturbing case of mistaken identity meant it was ground-up mummy that flew off apothecary shelves during the Middle Ages and up through the eighteenth century. And it wasn't just the mummy wrappings being ground up, either. Somewhere along the line, the term *mumia* started referring to the whole mummy—body, wrappings, and all.

It was this little—or rather ginormous—mix-up that gave mummies their name!

Once removed, the slippery, bloody organs were covered in natron, which was a naturally occurring salt substance. The natron dried out the organs—like how salt is used to dehydrate certain meats today—and then the organs were plopped into containers called canopic jars. The jars would be buried with the rest of the body. In case the mummy needed his liver in the afterlife.

The body itself was also blanketed with natron and allowed to dry for more than a month. Then the embalmer stuffed it with sawdust or straw or bandages to help it keep its shape. He covered it with oils and expensive, pleasant-smelling spices. Then the body was carefully wrapped in linens, finger by finger and toe by toe. Resin, the sap from pine trees, was often added to the wrappings to offer even more protection.

These newer, dehydrated mummies fared much better than the earlier ones. The embalmers were making progress. But they weren't done experimenting. They decided the brain had to go next.

Most often, brain removal was done by jamming an iron hook up the corpse's nose with enough force to break through the relatively weak bone standing between the nose and the brain. Once the hook was where it needed to be, some experts believe it was used to pull the brain out through the nose. Others disagree. They think the embalmer actually whisked the hook around and around and around—like how you might whip up some cake batter—which essentially turned the brain to mush. Then all the embalmer had to do was flip the body over, tilt the head down, and let the liquified brain pour right out through the nose.

Animal Mummies

The ancient Egyptians didn't stop with mummifying people. They also mummified a whole host of critters, including crocodiles, baboons, birds, fish, snakes, and even dung beetles.

In some cases, the mummified animals were beloved pets. The ancient Egyptians loved their pets and hoped to be reunited with them in the afterlife.

Sometimes a bird or chunk of meat was mummified and placed in a tomb to provide food for the dead.

In certain cases—such as the famous Apis bull—the mummified animal was a real standout. Revered and pampered throughout its life, the animal was considered sacred. Upon its death, priests and commoners alike mourned its loss, and it was carefully mummified.

But most of the animals mummified in ancient Egypt were intended as something called a votive offering. A pilgrim wanting to send a message to a god would travel to a temple and buy a mummified animal from a priest, such as a cat if they were seeking favor with the goddess Bastet, or an ibis if they were targeting the moon god, Thoth.

Once bought, the animal mummy, often along with a written message for the designated god, would be placed in a catacomb alongside animal mummies bought by other pilgrims. Incredibly, tombs have been found up and down the Nile containing hundreds, thousands, and sometimes *millions* of animal mummies.

This callous approach to the brain sounds quite odd, doesn't it? The embalmer took such care with the liver and intestines. Why not the brain?

Turns out the ancient Egyptians had no respect for the brain. It wasn't felt to be important. They believed the heart did all the thinking and feeling.

Over time the embalmers continued to experiment. They played around with the eyes, replacing them with stones or onions.

They tried sewing a corpse's fingernails in place before dehydrating the body so they wouldn't fall off as the fingers shrank.

Under the Wrappings

As we learned about in the "Animal Mummies" section, scores of pilgrims wanted to buy mummified animals to serve as votive offerings. So it's no surprise that the making and selling of these mummies became quite the business.

But mummifying an animal wasn't easy. It took time. It took patience. It took acquiring an animal in the first place.

Or did it?

As it turns out, the whole acquiring-an-animal part appears to have been optional. When a team of scientists from the University of Manchester studied more than eight hundred animal mummies, they discovered that one third of them were fakes. They contained no animal materials at all!

Thankfully the ancient Egyptian embalmers took the mummification of their fellow human beings much more seriously (reports that they occasionally created fake human mummies are most likely erroneous), but the same can unfortunately not be said for those coming after them. During the whole mummy-medicine craze in Europe (see "Mummy Medicine"), not all the ground-up mummy sold in apothecaries came from real ancient Egyptian specimens.

Sometimes newly dead bodies—often the bodies of criminals—were treated in such a way that they *looked* like ancient mummies. These fakes would then be bought, ground up, and sold to the unsuspecting sick.

They filled the bodies with new and different materials to see if they could get the bodies to better keep their shape. They varied how they wrapped the bodies and how they decorated them. They may have even added hair extensions!

Year after year, generation after generation, embalmers reached into bodies and yanked out organs. They turned brains into liquid mush and wrapped linens around dried, dehydrated noggins. Personally, I find it inspiring that through hard work and experimentation, mummy makers were able to create something so profoundly enduring. Well over a thousand years have passed since they last wrapped a body, and people are still gazing upon their work in fascination today.

Q: What did the ancient Egyptian embalmer say when he was feeling sad?

A: I want my mummy!

Mummy Madness

Over a thousand years have passed since mummies stopped being made in Egypt. And during this time, humans have found all kinds of interesting ways to use the dead bodies. One way was as a medicine (see "Mummy Medicine"), but the strangeness didn't stop there. Here are some other mummy uses:

• From the sixteenth century through the early twentieth century, mummies were ground up and turned into a paint with the ultra-descriptive name "Mummy Brown."

• In the nineteenth century, wealthy European citizens were known to obtain mummies for the sole purpose of unwrapping them. At parties. To impress their guests.

• "Mummy dust" was a potion ingredient used by the Evil Queen in Walt Disney's 1937 film *Snow White and the Seven Dwarfs*. She used it to make herself appear old.

• It has long been said that during the nineteenth century mummy wrappings were used to *make paper*. Is there any truth to this urban legend? Some experts say yes. Most aren't so sure.

• When a huge cache of cat mummies was discovered in 1888, about 180,000 of them were shipped to England where they were ground up. And used as fertilizer!

Chapter 2

For the Love of Leeches

Job: Leech Collector

Time Period: Middle Ages and Beyond

Leeches—with their suckered ends; slimy, sluglike bodies; and thirst for blood—are like the vampire bats of the water. Only worse. Vampire bats usually leave humans alone. Leeches? Not so much.

But for some people living in the Middle Ages, their very livelihoods depended on the little bloodsuckers. These people . . . were leech collectors.

The first thing you probably want to know is *why* people went around collecting leeches in the first place. Were they used for food? No. Were they kept as pets, like the Middle Ages' equivalent of a goldfish? Nope. That's not it either.

Leeches were collected so they could suck blood.

Out of sick people.

This might sound like something out of a bad horror novel, but medical healers living centuries ago didn't understand diseases the way we do now. They didn't know about viruses or bacteria. They didn't understand what caused diabetes or why some people suffered from leprosy while others did not.

This lack of knowledge caused physicians to have all kinds of beliefs about sickness and health that seem downright preposterous to us today. One of those bizarre beliefs was that a good way to make a sick person feel better was to get rid of their excess fluids.

Sometimes this fluid-eliminating process involved making the patient throw up. Sometimes the aim was to cause major diarrhea. But more often than not the fluid being removed was blood, and it was removed in a procedure known as bloodletting.

We don't know exactly when bloodletting first became a thing, but we do know it started a long, long time ago.

My Mom the Leech

Picture an animal that does a great job raising their young. What animal did you come up with? Humans? Dogs? Orangutans?

I bet leeches were not the first thing that popped into your head—or the hundredth—but the two-eyed flat leech actually doesn't do too bad a job on the parenting front. These leeches produce cocoons, which are little egg-containing packages, that get pressed right onto their bodies. The leeches will carry the cocoons around, protecting them from enemies and fanning them with their bodies.

Eventually the eggs will hatch, and out will come a bunch of tiny larval leeches. These little younglings attach to their parent using one of their suckers, and for weeks they'll get carted around everywhere. And if free transportation and protection from enemies aren't enough, the baby leeches also get a five-star meal plan. Anytime the parent leech catches some supper, they let their stuck-on babies get first dibs at all the blood.

Reading about this selfless leech parenting style almost makes you like leeches, doesn't it? Or maybe not.

Carvings in an Egyptian tomb dating to around 1500 BCE even seem to depict someone having their blood removed. Fast-forward to the Middle Ages and bloodletting was all the rage. Suffering from a stomachache? A headache? A sore throat? The cure was simple. Find someone willing to drain your blood and let them have at it.

Mosquito Misery

While leeches are very well known for their love of blood, where I live it's mosquitoes—not leeches—that reign supreme in the bloodsucking department. Their itchy, irritating bites are as much a part of summer as sunshine, grilling out, and trips to the lake.

But unlike leeches, mosquitoes don't go after blood because they're hungry. Mosquitoes get their energy from plant sugars, like nectar and fruit. The only reason mosquitoes even bother with blood is because they need the proteins in it for egg production.

Because male mosquitoes don't make eggs, they live a 100 percent blood-free life. They don't even have the mouthparts needed to suck blood, should they ever get the hankering to see what all the fuss is about.

So ultimately it's the female mosquitoes you have to watch out for. They're the ones that cover you in annoyingly itchy bumps. They're the ones that ruined your

Boy Scout camping trip last year. And they're the ones that are brilliant at spreading illnesses—like yellow fever and malaria. It's difficult to imagine given their minuscule size, but mosquitoes are so good at infecting people with fatal diseases that they are considered the deadliest animal on the planet.

RHONDA, IS THAT YOU? HOW ARE YOU, GIRL!?

SLUUUURRP

Bloodletting could be done with a sharp rock. A knife. A lancet.

Or a leech.

And this was where the resident leech collector entered the picture. Countless people depended on them for the leeches they so sorely desired.

A leech collector's job was to wade out into the boggy marshes with their arms and legs bare. Like the earthworm dangling at the end of a fisherman's hook, their body was the bait. As absurd as this might sound, they wanted the little suckers to chomp down on their skin. Heck, they might even wiggle around a bit as they made their way through the bogs. Leeches, which can sense motion, would feel the movement and come investigate.

The leech collector's target was a specific species of leech called the European medicinal leech. This leech—with the fancy scientific name *Hirudo medicinalis*—has two suckers, one on each end. It also has thirty-two "brains," ten stomachs, and three powerful jaws lined with hundreds of itty-bitty teeth called denticles.

When one of these leeches decided to gnaw on a leech collector's leg, it raked its denticles back and forth, back and forth, back and forth against the skin like a saw cutting into a piece of wood. After its three jaws finished making a Y-shaped cut, it sucked. And sucked. And sucked the blood.

This might sound super painful, but it wasn't. Leech saliva contains an anesthetic that makes a leech bite relatively painless. On the surface this seems thoughtful of the little leech, especially if you compare it to the not-so-painless bite of a hungry crocodile or angry grizzly bear. But the leech has a selfish reason for causing no pain: It wants to feed in peace.

Talk About a Fast

Most humans living in the United States eat two or three meals a day, often with a snack or two or five thrown in for good measure. While we *could* go several weeks without food if necessary, doing so would make most of us cranky.

But there are animals that can go an amazingly long time without a meal in their tummy. Animals like the European medicinal leech. They're able to go an entire year between meals!

And leeches aren't alone. Crocodiles and Galápagos tortoises can also go a year without eating. Lungfish can go three to five years between meals. And that's still nothing compared to tardigrades.

Tardigrades—also called water bears or moss piglets—are eight-legged critters that are usually no longer than a millimeter. But what they lack in size they make up for in toughness. They can survive for short periods of time in environments colder than −327 degrees Fahrenheit and as hot as 300 degrees Fahrenheit. They can live at the bottom of the deepest ocean and up in outer space. And if need be, they can go *decades* without any food or water!

WE COULD TRY THAT NEW THAI PLACE.

NAH, I'M STUFFED— BIG LUNCH LAST FEBRUARY.

If its bite hurt, it would alert its victim to its presence. And considering that leeches often feed on animals that would happily chow down on a leech supper, it wouldn't take much for the tables to be turned. And the leech would no longer be the one getting the full belly. (Or the full *bellies*, considering the whole ten stomachs thing.)

While the ouch-less bite was nice for the leech collector, it didn't change the fact that their goal was to get covered in the slimy creatures. And after they succeeded, next they needed to get the leeches off. One way to do this was to wait. Once a leech got a full blood meal it would simply let go and fall off. But this could take a while, and what if the leech collector failed to catch the leech before it plopped back into the water? It was much quicker to just peel the little suckers off.

After spending a day removing leech after leech from their body, the leech collector's fun was still not over. Now they got to spend the next several hours walking around with blood streaming down their arms and legs. This was because anesthetics are not the only chemicals found in leech saliva. The saliva also contains powerful anticoagulants—whose job it is to keep blood flowing by preventing it from clotting or clumping up.

Between the blood the leeches sucked up and the blood that continued oozing long after they were gone, it didn't take long before the leech collector was running low on the red stuff.

Their skin started looking beluga whale pale. They'd feel faint. Dizzy. Sick. And every time they waded back into the germ-infested waters with open sores all over, it was an invitation for infection . . . which could make them feel even crummier.

Leech Mania!

This chapter obviously focuses on leech collecting during the Middle Ages, but did the use of leeches end with the start of the Renaissance? Definitely not. In fact, it was quite the opposite. Things actually peaked in the early 1800s when French physician François-Joseph-Victor Broussais (1772–1838) ushered in a time referred to as "leech mania." Even more than the bloodletting-loving physicians before him, Broussais believed leeches could cure everything.

During his heyday, *millions* of leeches were used every year in France alone. Add in the leeches used in England and Germany and the rest of Europe, and the poor leeches were driven almost to extinction.

To get through the day, a leech collector probably told themself the same thing over and over again: *Sure, my job is wet and dirty and miserable. It's slimy and bloody and makes me feel sick. The pay is horrible. But at least I'm helping the sick get better.*

Or were they?

The sad truth is, bloodletting wasn't a magic bullet against the common cold. It didn't eliminate migraines or mental illness or fevers. Instead of helping people live better or longer, leeches and bloodletting only succeeded in stripping people of their precious, life-giving blood. Meaning leech collectors actually brought patients one step closer to death.

And that's a truth that sucks even more than the leeches.

Q: Why did the boy keep a leech as a pet?
A: Because it was so attached to him!

Leeches to the Rescue

Considering that bloodletting with leeches did more harm than good, it seems a fair bet that leeches were tossed out of medicine long ago. Doctors like to *fix* their patients. Not hurt them.

But astonishingly, leeches are still used in medicine today, albeit in a very different way. Let's consider an example. Your dad is teaching you knife safety in the kitchen when he accidentally lops off a finger. Whoops! Your mother races him to a hospital where a hand surgeon works tirelessly to join up the bones and sew together his tendons, arteries, veins, and nerves as best she can. She does a top-notch job.

But as often happens when a body part has been surgically reattached, your dad's veins—which are the blood vessels that act as superhighways for blood traveling from his finger back to his heart—don't work very well at first. They're sluggish. It's as though there's been a major finger-vein traffic jam.

This is a problem because blood can still flow *out* to his finger through his arteries, the blood just can't go back. More and more blood pools in his finger. If this pooling continues for long, his finger will die.

But wait! There's still hope. It's time to call in the leeches.

Leeches are placed on his finger, and they go to work sucking up all the pooled blood. Their actions buy his veins time to heal and work properly again. Yay leeches!

For saving your dad's finger, you'd hope the leeches would be presented with a medal. A trophy. A key to the city. Or they'd at least get the chance to live out their remaining leechy days in a nice, cozy retirement marsh somewhere. But alas, the Food and Drug Administration considers leeches to be single-use. Which means their reward for saving your dad's finger is their own death.

Chapter 3

A Jack of All Trades

Job: Barber-Surgeon

Time Period: Middle Ages Through the Renaissance

Where would you go if your hair needed a trim? To a salon or barber shop, right?

And if your head hurt so badly it felt like it might explode? You'd ring up your doctor.

Left leg infected and need to be cut off? It's time to find yourself a good surgeon.

And if you have an excruciating toothache, you'd better schedule an appointment with your dentist.

These four jobs—barber, doctor, surgeon, and dentist—are not the same thing. If you buck tradition and ask your surgeon to cut your hair, you risk ending up a laughingstock at school the next day. Ask your dentist to cut off your leg? Well . . . let's not think about that one too much.

During the Middle Ages and Renaissance, though, a single person—called a barber-surgeon—fulfilled all these roles. And as odd as it might sound, the way this job came to be actually makes a wee bit of sense. You see, during the medieval period, a sick or injured person only had so many places they could go for help:

- **Their garden. It's possible an herb growing there might offer some relief.**

- **Religion. In medieval Europe, the Church was top dog. The big cheese. The head honcho. It influenced every aspect of life. Therefore, many people looked to the Church first when they were feeling ill. A clergyman could offer prayers. Recommend a penance. Suggest a saint to appeal to for help. Some monks even performed blood-letting and simple surgeries . . . until the Church put an end to that.**

- A folk healer, like the neighborhood wise woman. She'd use some combination of potions, medications, prayers, incantations, bloodletting, and magic. Her treatments could be made from mundane ingredients like herbs and vegetable roots. Or they might contain snails. Animal dung. Leeches. Or the brains, spleen, liver, and fat of dead animals.

- An apothecary. Maybe some dried-up mummy would do the trick.

- A physician. Though, to be honest, medieval doctors weren't all that helpful. They were few in number, super expensive, and they spent most of their time strolling around in fancy robes deciding what was wrong with a person by analyzing urine samples or studying the placement of the planets and stars in the sky. Occasionally a physician would stoop as low as to take a pulse, but many refused to touch their patients at all.

A Witch Hunt

Most of the time if you excel at your job it's a good thing. But this wasn't always the case for wise women living at the end of the medieval period. If they were too successful at healing the people who came knocking at their door, it could be dangerous.

Why would this be?

The Middle Ages were a time when both religion *and* superstition ruled the day. There was an interesting hodgepodge of beliefs: Illness was frequently assumed to come from either God or the devil, and yet toothaches were thought to be caused by little worms called toothworms, and there is evidence that some people believed in elfsickness—a disease caused by miniature arrows being shot by tiny, invisible elves.

In this weird soup of beliefs, if a wise woman's potions, herbs, and incantations worked *too* well, people started to think she must be in cahoots with the devil. In other words, she must be a witch.

Ultimately this helped contribute to the horrific witch hunts that started at the end of the Middle Ages and continued for hundreds of years. It got so bad during the sixteenth and seventeenth centuries that the number of "witches" put to death in Europe numbered in the tens of thousands!

Theriac: A Medieval Cure-All

People living in the medieval period would ideally never get sick. Never get injured. Never find themselves in the hands of a physician, a barber-surgeon, or a folk healer. But at some point almost everyone needed medical attention. If they were lucky, they'd simply be given a medicine—such as an herbal tea, a potion concocted by the local wise woman, or something bought at the local apothecary—like theriac.

Theriac was to the Middle Ages what ibuprofen is today. It was everywhere. The exact recipe varied from town to town and apothecary to apothecary. A batch took longer than a year to make and could contain more than eighty ingredients. Ingredients like viper flesh, opium, spices, vinegar, wine, honey, and mummy dust.

In ancient times, theriac was used as an antidote to poisons, like snake bites, but by the Middle Ages it—along with bloodletting—was seemingly used to cure e-v-e-r-y-t-h-i-n-g. Have heart problems? Seizures? Arthritis? Having a hard time sleeping? Having a hard time pooping? No worries. Just get yourself some theriac!

Considering these options, it's clear that not all medical needs were being met—especially for patients who needed hands-on help. So who answered this call? The hair-trimming, beard-shaving barbers! Barbers were already experienced with a blade, after all, and they realized there was money to be made if they could expand their list of services. And really, how much harder could it be to cut off an arm than to tame an unruly cowlick?

Initially the main medical procedure barbers (or barber-surgeons, as barbers who dabbled in the medical world were called) performed was bloodletting. They sliced open veins and applied bloodsucking leeches. To advertise this new service, a barber-surgeon might place a bowl of fresh blood in his shop window or hang bloody bandages outside his door. Charming, right?

With time, barber-surgeons started doing more and more. Like yanking teeth, changing wound dressings, and slicing off warts and cancerous growths. Many offered limb-chopping-off services for those who needed a limb chopped off. Some even removed bladder stones and performed eye surgery.

Unfortunately, though, a trip to a barber-surgeon's shop wasn't without risk.

Unlike surgeons in the twenty-first century who undergo years of hard-core medical training, most barber-surgeons had no formal school education. They learned their trade by apprenticing.

The Islamic East Rules the Day

When the Roman Empire fell in 476 CE, Europe was plunged into the Middle Ages, a period once believed to be so terrible that it was referred to as the Dark Ages. We've subsequently learned that the Middle Ages got something of a bum rap, but even so, it was a time where throughout Europe progress in just about every field slowed to a sloth's pace. And sometimes went backward.

It's easy to generalize and assume the entire medieval world was stuck, but this assumption would be wrong. While Europe was floundering like a snail without its shell, large areas of the world were flourishing. In the Middle East and Western Asia, education and learning were valued. Huge advancements were made in art, science, and medicine. Ancient medical writings—like those of Hippocrates and Galen—were preserved, translated, studied, and built upon.

In Europe, the Middle Ages were a period of relative stagnation. In the East, they were a golden age!

And barber-surgeons didn't worry about sanitizing their tools or keeping work surfaces clean. They didn't think twice about using the same bloody knife on person after person. They—like all healers of the time—had no idea their dirty hands and equipment made it more likely that their patients would get an infection. And considering that antibiotics wouldn't be discovered until the 1900s, infections were often fatal.

A trip to a barber-surgeon could also be very painful, given the annoying lack of good anesthesia. Some patients got drunk before knocking on a barber-surgeon's door, hoping the alcohol would numb their pain. Some were given a natural painkiller, like opium—ideally in a dose high enough to decrease their suffering without, you know, killing them. And many patients got nothing at all; they'd simply be held or strapped down while the barber-surgeon pulled out his tools and did his thing.

While a trip to the barber-surgeon was risky and often painful for the patient, what about the barber-surgeon himself? Let's envision an imaginary day in *his* shoes:

8 a.m. Mr. Thompson strolls through the door needing his hair trimmed and beard shaved. If the barber-surgeon could also pick out all the lice, that would be great.

8:30 a.m. Mr. Smith comes in with breath so bad it could scare away a skunk. He needs an abscessed tooth pulled.

9 a.m. Mrs. Baker needs a cataract taken care of. Easy peasy. Just takes a needle to the eyeball.

9:30 a.m. Another beard trim. With lice removal, of course.

10 a.m. Mrs. Hall has a splitting headache. If the barber-surgeon would please apply some slimy leeches, she'd be forever grateful.

10:30 a.m. Mr. Walker waddles in with a massive boil on his bum. The barber-surgeon lances it (cuts it open), sending an impressive eruption of rotten-smelling pus flying across the room.

LUNCH

12:30 p.m. Eight-year-old William Cooper has a badly broken leg that needs to be set. By 12:35, the barber-surgeon would happily exchange his right pinky toe for some noise-canceling headphones.

1:00 p.m. A hair trim.

1:30 p.m. Mrs. Rolfe is feeling peaky. She'd like a quick bloodletting.

2:00 p.m. The entire Wood family swarms in. They're unhappy that Grandpa died at home yesterday after his rotten tooth was removed. Something about it bleeding. And bleeding. And bleeding.

3:00 p.m. In wander a haircut and a bloodletting at the same time. Plop on some leeches. Trim away. Everyone's happy. Especially the leeches.

4:00 p.m. Mr. Webb's son half carries, half drags his father

36

through the door. The old man is burning up with a fever. He's calling for his mother, who died twenty years ago. His arm is bright red and oozing pus. The barber-surgeon collects his full payment and then starts cutting off the arm. He knows Mr. Webb probably won't live through the procedure. And he's right.

What a day. Noisy. Nauseating. Smelly. Heartbreaking. And after all that hard work, barber-surgeons didn't even get much respect. Physicians looked down at them. They were frequently the butt of jokes. Many considered them little more than butchers.

But for injured medieval peasants with nowhere else to turn, barber-surgeons often saved the day. It's a beard-trimmer. It's a tooth-puller. It's a leech-applier. No! It's a barber-surgeon!

Q: How did the barber-surgeon make sure his patient didn't get too sad after he chopped off her arm?

A: He left her funny bone.

A Little Hole in the Head

During the Middle Ages, most medical practitioners shied away from performing invasive surgeries, like removing appendixes and gallstone-filled gallbladders. And considering their lack of knowledge about anatomy, anesthesia, and infection, this was undoubtedly a good call.

Oddly, though, barber-surgeons didn't have the same hesitation about cutting into a person's skull. When deemed necessary, they'd perform a surgery called trepanning, in which part of the skull bone was removed to expose the

surface of the brain. Looking further back in time, you'll discover that trepanning was actually conducted by ancient societies all across the globe, even more than seven thousand years ago!

Throughout history trepanning was performed by different people for different reasons. It could be done to release pressure on the brain after a bad bonk to the head. To treat headaches or seizures. To "cure" mental illness. And some religious leaders performed trepanation to get rid of demons.

Archeological evidence suggests that not only did many people survive this surgery, some had it performed more than once!

Ambroise Paré: The Be-All and End-All in Barber-Surgeoning

The most famous of all barber-surgeons was Ambroise Paré. Growing up in France in the sixteenth century, Paré spent much of his early career on bloody battlefields taking care of gunshot wound after gruesome gunshot wound. Like all barber-surgeons of his day, Paré dealt with these terrible injuries in about the most barbaric manner imaginable: by pouring *boiling hot oil* into the wounds!

Why would barber-surgeons do that? They reckoned the hot oil would stop the bleeding and simultaneously counteract the poison they assumed was in gunpowder. They were trying to *help* the soldier, but it's hard to imagine a pain worse than having boiling hot anything poured into an open, inflamed sore.

Then one day Paré was faced with so many gunshot wounds that he ran out of oil. Needing to do *something* for the remaining soldiers, he made a paste out of egg yolks, turpentine, and rose oil and slathered the mixture on instead.

In the morning, the soldiers who'd received the boiling oil treatment were just like they always were: writhing in pain.

Feverish. And sporting red, inflamed, ugly wounds.

Those on the receiving end of his salve, on the other hand, were far more comfortable. Their wounds were healing!

And just like that, a new, better, more humane way to deal with gunshot wounds was discovered.

Paré's contribution to medicine and surgery didn't end there, either. He came up with better ways to perform amputations. He invented new surgical tools. He created prostheses for people who'd lost body parts.

Ambroise Paré might have been a mere barber-surgeon, a profession ridiculed by many, but he sure got the last laugh. Not only did he serve four different kings, but many consider him to be the father of modern surgery!

Chapter 4

The Dead Rise

Job: Resurrection Men

Time Period: Eighteenth and Nineteenth Centuries

There's no doubt about it . . . it's *hard* when someone you love dies. We want Grandma, Grandpa, and Great-Aunt Petunia to live forever. To always be there sneaking us candy, telling us stories, and squeezing our cheeks. Okay, so maybe not the cheeks part. But the rest of it for sure.

Then there's the heartbreaking burial. If you've ever watched a casket get lowered into the ground and covered with dirt, you know it feels so . . . final. There's no coming back from that.

Unless, of course, Great-Aunt Petunia is secretly a vampire. Or a zombie. *Or* you happen to live in nineteenth-century England. Because in nineteenth-century England, there was no guarantee that Great-Aunt Petunia would stay buried in the ground where you left her. A resurrection man might have other plans for her.

Now normally when we hear the word "resurrection" we think of a dead person being brought back to life. Like in *Tangled* how Rapunzel cries and voilà—Eugene is alive! Or in *The Lord of the Rings* when Gandalf magically returns from certain death. But the resurrection man who has his sights set on your Great-Aunt Petunia isn't planning to bring her back to life. He merely wants to dig up her still-dead body.

And sell it!

At this point, you're undoubtedly wondering who would want to buy Great-Aunt Petunia's rotting corpse. The answer: doctors. Yup. The very people who help you feel better when you're sick used to pay *real money* for dead, dug-up bodies.

On the surface this makes no sense. So let's dig deeper.

In order for doctors and surgeons to do their job, it helps if they know what the inside of a human body looks like. Where the liver is. How the blood vessels connect to the heart. What a normal kidney looks like. It's hard to remove a burst appendix, after all, if you have no idea what an appendix is. Or where it lies within the body.

Family Love

When the death of a family member occurs, we all deal with the loss in different ways. Some of us get depressed. Some get angry. Some go into denial. But most of us wouldn't react like William Harvey.

Harvey was an English surgeon and anatomy specialist whose main claim to fame was discovering how the human circulatory system works—meaning he figured out how the heart and blood vessels were connected.

ALL RIGHT, FATHER, TIME FOR YOUR MEDICINE.

Harvey's fierce dedication to the study of human anatomy was never clearer than when his father and sister died. Harvey didn't have their bodies buried. Or cremated. He didn't send them plunging over a waterfall in a birchbark canoe.

Nope.

Harvey plopped their bodies right onto his very own dissection table!

For much of medical history, though, doctors had to get by without this knowledge. This is because dissecting (or cutting up) a dead human body was considered a major no-no. Now admittedly there were *some* anatomy textbooks out there. Like that of Galen, a famous physician living during the days of the ancient Roman Empire. But if performing dissections wasn't allowed, where did Galen get his information?

For a while he acted as a physician to the gladiators. When gladiators came to him with ripped-off limbs and gaping stomach wounds, Galen scrutinized their insides as best he could while trying to patch them up. Even more of his knowledge was gained by dissecting nonhuman animals, from pigs to monkeys to lizards to camels. But as we all know, the insides of a rat or dog or fish are not the same as the insides of a person.

A human heart has four chambers. A lizard heart has three. A camel has three stomach compartments, we only have one. A human kidney looks like a bean, while horses have a heart-shaped kidney. And so on. And so forth.

For centuries, doctors studied Galen's books as though they were *The Ultimate Handbook of Anatomy and Medicine*. Questioning him wasn't allowed. Questioning him could get you thrown in jail.

But eventually, doctors came to realize that much of what Galen wrote about anatomy was wrong. And he slid right off the anatomy pedestal.

But now what? Well, fortunately, in 1482, Pope Sixtus IV did the unthinkable. He declared dissections to be A-OK— as long as the body was that of an executed criminal. Over time, public dissections became a major attraction. Anyone who could afford a ticket could watch a dead body get chopped up at a tavern, a public hall, or an anatomy amphitheater.

Now that the general public could watch dissections, though, it obviously became expected that medical students and doctors participate in dissections as well. Private anatomy schools popped up all over Europe to teach wannabe doctors about the human body.

And this is when the problem truly began, especially in the United Kingdom. Laws there still prohibited the dissection of anyone other than executed criminals, and there weren't enough of those to go around.

Anatomy schools became desperate. If they didn't have enough cadavers, they couldn't teach anatomy. They'd have to close their doors. It was bye-bye profits. But lucky for them, resurrection men—also called resurrectionists, body snatchers, or sack-'em-up men—were more than happy to help out.

Most of the time resurrection men got their bodies by digging up fresh graves. Fresh because medical students didn't exactly fancy the idea of examining rotten, liquified, stinking bodies.

Dissection Today

As you might imagine, medical students still study anatomy. And while there *are* fancy 3D models and interactive computer programs available, many medical schools still use human bodies. There is nothing like learning on the real thing.

Students dissect out each facial nerve and major artery. They see with their own eyes where the various leg muscles connect to bone. They tug on tendons and watch how the fingers move in response. They hold a brain, a liver, a heart in their hands.

The bodies medical students learn from today are thankfully not dug out of the ground in the dark of night. They are donated. Just like some people donate their organs after death, others make the decision to give their entire body to a medical school.

As a doctor, *I* dissected a body during medical school. And while it was disturbing at first to cut into a real human being, the entire experience was profoundly moving. It was incredible to know that someone donated their body so that I could become a better doctor.

I was never told the name of the gentleman I dissected. They keep that information private. But to each and every donor out there: I thank you!

Taking Things Up a Notch

With digging up graves being such filthy and dangerous work, some people found easier ways to get their hands on bodies to sell. Most famous among them were William Burke and William Hare. These guys didn't wait for people to drop dead; they did the dirty work themselves. They smothered or strangled at least sixteen people in the 1820s and sold their bodies to Dr. Robert Knox at the University of Edinburgh.

When William Burke's murderous ways were finally detected, he was sentenced to death and hanged in 1829. After death, he sure got his comeuppance when his own body ended up on a dissection table. What happened to

GOODNESS, BURKE, HOW DO YOU FIND THEM SO FRESH?

HEH... HEH... JUST A COINCIDENCE.

Burke's body after that? His skeleton was put on display at the University of Edinburgh Anatomical Museum, and a pocketbook made from his skin (yes, his skin!) was placed in the Edinburgh's Surgeons' Hall Museum.

No pocketbook was ever made out of William Hare, though. He testified against Burke.

And went free.

The resurrection men would watch graveyards for funerals. They'd pay graveyard guards to point them toward the newest bodies. Often, the graveyard workers became body snatchers themselves.

The job of resurrection men was dirty. It was smelly. It was fouler than foul. They had to handle the dead bodies of skeletal-thin old people who'd died after years of illness. And chubby-cheeked toddlers who'd succumbed to childhood diseases. And factory workers who'd died in gruesome accidents.

Their job also wasn't easy. Because surprise, surprise, Great-Uncle Bob didn't want Great-Aunt Petunia to be dug up and sold off. He wanted her to stay in the ground where she belonged. To protect her he might have had her buried extra deep, so the resurrection men had to work harder to get to her. Or he could pay big bucks to bury her in an iron coffin. He could arrange for a large iron contraption—called a mortsafe—to be placed above her grave. He might wait to bury her until her body had already become putrid, thus making her body near-worthless to the local body snatcher. Or maybe Great-Uncle Bob hung out at the cemetery night after night keeping watch. Gun in hand.

Even with all the obstacles in their way, resurrection men robbed graveyards and sold off bodies until the Anatomy Act of 1832 was passed in the United Kingdom. This law made it legal for doctors to cut up any corpse that wasn't claimed by friends or family, like the bodies of the poor souls who died in workhouses.

Many welcomed the Anatomy Act. It meant their Great-Aunt Petunias were safe. Some hated the law because it was unfair to those who were poor, friendless, and family-less. But nobody hated the Anatomy Act as much as the resurrection men. Because it meant their dug-up bodies were no longer needed.

And they were out of a job.

Q: How did the resurrection man know that the body he'd dug up was still alive?

A: It kept coffin!

Let's Talk Money

Why would anyone want to be a resurrection man? Who would want to sneak out in the dead of night, break into cemeteries, and dig up corpses? Who would want to deal with the constant threat of encountering the armed and angry family members of the deceased?

Well, gruesome as the job was, there were some perks. First of all, resurrection men got their summers off. Nobody wanted to dissect a body in the heat of summer. The stench would have been out of this world.

The other perk? Money. Cold, hard cash. Even with their shortened work year, resurrection men earned several times more than other unskilled workers of their day.

Not only that, but even if they messed up and accidentally dug up a body that was so rotten nobody would want to dissect it, they could still make money by plucking out the teeth and selling them.

To dentists.

To be made into dentures!

The Unsavory Side of a Medical Education

Bill of Tuition

SCHOOL YEAR: 1876
AMOUNT DUE: £40
STATUS: PAID

Paying resurrection men for bodies was super expensive, so some eighteenth-century anatomy instructors sought other ways to get their hands on dug-up remains. Like by sending their own students out to the cemeteries.

Late-night grave-robbing sprees were *encouraged* at many schools. There was even an anatomy school in Scotland where students could supposedly pay their tuition with corpses!

Chapter 5

Watching the Dead Rot

Job: Watchman at a Waiting Mortuary
Time Period: Nineteenth Century

Nightmare alert! This chapter deals with people getting buried. *Alive!*

Here's a question for you: What is your single greatest fear? Heights? Tornados? Failing your end-of-semester math test?

If you lived in Europe during the eighteenth or nineteenth century, there's a good chance your greatest fear would have been being buried alive. That you'd be declared dead. Your body would be put in a coffin. You'd be buried. And *then* you'd wake up. Because you hadn't actually died.

People just *thought* you had.

But now that you were six feet underground in a dark, tiny box with no food, no water, and almost no air, it wouldn't be long before you *were* dead.

Man. What an awful way to go!

Famous Fears

Taphephobia: the fear of being buried alive. Many famous people suffered from it.

Like George Washington. Some of his last words were to his secretary, asking that his body not be placed in its vault until three days after he was declared dead.

And Alfred Nobel—the inventor of dynamite and the man behind the Nobel Prize. He was *not* coming awake in a coffin. His last will and testament ended with the following sentence: "Finally, it is my express wish that following my death, my arteries be severed, and when this has been done and competent doctors have confirmed clear signs of death, my remains be incinerated in a crematorium."

Then there was Frédéric Chopin, the famous music composer. Apparently, his last recorded written words were "swear to make them cut me open, so I won't be buried alive."

And finally there's Hans Christian Andersen, the author of such stories as *The Ugly Duckling* and *The Snow Queen*. He was so terrified of being wrongly assumed dead that he would go to sleep with a piece of paper next to his bed saying, "I only appear to be dead."

Nowadays it sounds strange to fear being buried alive. Thanks to modern medical technology, we are really, really, really, *really* good at *not* burying still-living people. But during the nineteenth century, everywhere a person turned they'd find horrific accounts of the latest poor soul to have suffered this fate.

Stories like that of a pregnant woman from Sweden. The night she was buried, the church caretaker heard awful moans and groans coming from her grave. Rather than find the closest shovel, the guy raced home and hid under his blankets. He was afraid the sounds were coming from a ghost.

Come morning, the caretaker told the church rector all about his terrifying, middle-of-the-night ghost encounter. The horrified rector immediately had the coffin dug back up. As the lid was pried off, the sight meeting all the eagerly awaiting eyes would have given anyone nightmares. They figured the poor women must have been buried alive because sometime during the night, all alone in her dark coffin, she'd given birth to her child.

Even more sad, by the time the coffin was opened, both mother and baby had died. For real.

And this was just one of many such stories. Some people at the time estimated that as many as one in ten people who were buried were put into the ground while still alive. Supporting these numbers were countless graves that were dug up only to find that the buried person had a contorted, pained expression on their face. Or their limbs were all folded up, as though they'd died while trying to push open a sealed coffin. Or their fingers had been chewed off—presumably self-inflicted by a person driven mad with terror.

Was Premature Burial
Really a Thing?

So were people *really* being buried alive during the nineteenth century? Unfortunately, yes. There were well-documented cases of people being buried alive.

What is unclear is how *often* it occurred. Many of the horrific stories of premature burials were just that: stories. Or exagger-ations. After all, on a slow-news day, what journalist wanted to fill his column with tales of Mr. Frank's runaway pig? Or Miss Smith's throat infection? No reader wanted to read about that.

Except Mr. Frank and Miss Smith.

So instead, the journalist would astonish his readers with news of the latest—most likely exaggerated—burial mess-up.

But what about the dug-up graves that genuinely looked like a person had been buried alive? Like our pregnant woman from this chapter. The one who was moaning in her grave and was ultimately found to have delivered her own baby. Incredibly, there is a scientific explanation for all of this. As a body decomposes, gas builds up in the abdomen.

If this gas escapes through the throat, it can produce a groaning sound. And if enough gas builds up? It can expel an unborn baby!

What about the bodies with chewed-off fingers, then? What possible explanation could there be for *that*? The answer: rodents. Before the coffins were set in their final resting place, rodents gnawed into the coffins and had themselves a little finger sandwich.

And what about the corpses found to have grimacing faces? Or the ones with the contracted arms and legs? According to Jan Bondeson, PhD, in the book *Buried Alive*, neither of these findings were "inconsistent with the natural composition of the body after death."

Bottom line: We know premature burials occurred. But did they occur as often as people feared they did?

Thank goodness, no!

As if these stories weren't scary enough, many doctors of the time readily admitted they weren't sure how to tell when a person was 100 percent, no-doubt-about-it, I'd-bet-my-life-on-it dead.

Premature burials became a *major* topic of conversation. And as doctors and laymen argued over the best way to know when a person was truly dead, a well-respected physician in Weimar, Germany—Dr. Christoph Wilhelm Hufeland—lent his support to those who believed the only way to be completely positive a person was dead was to wait for clear-cut evidence of decomposition.

In other words, to wait until you saw the body rotting!

Dr. Hufeland wanted buildings—called "houses of the dead" or "waiting mortuaries"—to be built in every German town and city. People would be taken to these waiting mortuaries upon death and be monitored 24/7 for any sign of life. No burial would occur until the body had started decaying.

The first waiting mortuary was built in Weimar, Germany, in the early 1790s. Berlin followed in 1795. Then Brunswick, Kassel, Mainz, Munich, and numerous other German and a few non-German cities followed suit.

Each waiting mortuary was a little different. Some were simple structures that looked like a run-of-the-mill house from the outside. Others were columned, architectural masterpieces built out of marble. Some of the mortuaries separated men from women. Others separated rich from poor. There were waiting mortuaries that were closed to the public. Others allowed tourists to pay a fee, come inside, and wander among the dead.

But every waiting mortuary had two things in common. First, they all smelled.

And second, they were all manned by a watchman whose job it was to watch the dead for signs of life.

Determining Death Without a Waiting Mortuary

Most towns and villages in the nineteenth century did not have a waiting mortuary. So how was death determined in those places?

One option was still to wait for a body to rot, only the waiting happened in homes. This doesn't sound like a *terrible* idea.

Unless you consider the stench.

Alternatively, doctors could look for evidence of breathing or a beating heart. But given the tools available to them at the time, these practices weren't 100 percent infallible.

Doctors and laymen alike therefore proposed countless methods for determining death. Most of these strategies were designed to cause such distress that—were a body *actually* alive—it would be compelled to show some sign of life. Here is a taste of the techniques used:

- Bugle loudly into the deceased's ear or surround them with horrific screeching.

- Jab them with needles or set razors to their feet.

- Stick a crawling insect into their ear.

- Jab a hot poker up their butt. Or, instead of a hot poker, blow tobacco smoke up their rear end.

- Cut off a finger or toe.

- Use the tongue-pulling method, my personal favorite. Here's the idea: After a person died, you'd grab their tongue and yank. Hard. You'd yank on it again. And again. And again. *For three hours!*

Eventually Dr. J. V. Laborde, the mastermind behind the whole tongue-pulling idea, invented a hand-cranked tongue-pulling machine. Instead of yanking on the tongue yourself, you'd turn a crank and the tongue would be pulled for you. Then you'd turn the crank again. And again. And again. *For three hours!*

Before we get into all the gross aspects of the watchman's job, I should first point out that there were some good things about the position. It was an indoor job. It didn't require much education. It wasn't labor intensive. And . . .

Hmmm . . .

Well, I guess that's it. There *were* no other good things about being a mortuary watchman.

In most waiting mortuaries, the watchman spent the majority of his time in a small, windowed room that looked out upon rows and rows of corpses. But he couldn't hide in that room all day long crocheting scarves. He periodically had to step out amid the cadavers. He'd clean around the beds in an effort to keep the smell down. He'd weave between the bodies, his senses alert. He'd watch for the slightest movement. Listen for the quietest groan or whimper. Sniff the air for the stench of decay.

Lovely, huh?

Watchmen were typically aided in their work by contraptions designed to make it nearly impossible for them to miss a reanimated body. Usually this aid took the form of a string that connected a finger or toe from each corpse to a noise-making device—like a bell. Thanks to this setup, anytime a body moved or shifted or quivered, the bell would chime.

During the day, a ringing bell might bring a twinge of excitement. A sliver of hope. Was the watchman about to see a dead man rise? Was he about to become a hero?

But imagine being woken by the clanging of a bell in the middle of a dark, stormy night. As lightning flashed and thunder crashed, the watchman had to creep into a room full of waxen dead corpses. To see if any were now alive.

The Safety Coffin

Given how much people feared being buried alive during the nineteenth century, it's no surprise that inventors throughout Europe and the United States started creating and patenting "safety coffins." While each safety coffin design was different, the general idea was the same: If they worked as intended, they'd give a falsely buried person a shot at rescue.

One of the most well known of these safety coffins was invented in the late 1800s by a man with an awesome name: Count Karnicé-Karnicki. His design included a tube, about 3.5 inches in diameter, that extended from inside the coffin up to an iron box located above the ground. A glass ball was placed on the corpse's chest, and any movement of the body triggered a spring-loaded mechanism that caused the iron box to burst open.

The opening of the box allowed air to rush into the coffin, it caused a bell to ring for approximately thirty minutes, and it released a waving flag. According to some reports, it even turned on an electric lamp. Assuming the graveyard attendant wasn't asleep on the job, he'd hear the bell, see the flag, and know it was time to find a shovel.

Even though lots of safety coffins were designed over the years, their sales weren't great. Many shied away because

they feared the coffin wouldn't work. They worried that the device would be activated, the breathing tube would open, but no flag would fly. No bell would chime. So nobody would know there was a person in need of being dug up.

So in time the person would still end up dying. The torture would just be drawn out, thanks to the air.

Others worried the mechanism would be triggered too easily—that built-up gas in a run-of-the-mill decomposing corpse would set things off. One could only imagine the poor graveyard attendant who was forced to dig up putrefied body after putrefied body as he followed the flags and ringing bells.

One might assume the bells would rarely ring, but, alas, this was not the case. Because when dead bodies start to decompose, they settle. They swell. *They move.*

Which caused bell after bell after bell to ring. Even in the middle of dark, stormy nights.

Given how dreadful and smelly the job of watchman was, it already seems like a pretty lousy occupation. But it doesn't end there. While on shift a watchman wasn't allowed to leave the building, not even for a second, without permission. Some mortuaries didn't allow them to curse or smoke while working. They weren't allowed visitors, who might serve as a distraction.

And while many mortuaries allowed the watchman to sleep while on night duty, others did not. To keep the watchman alert and . . . well . . . watching, some observation rooms had no bed. No table. No chair.

Taking this you-must-stay-ever-alert philosophy one step further, in a Frankfurt mortuary, the watchman had to crank a handle every half hour or a loud alarm would go off and broadcast to anyone listening that the watchman had fallen asleep on the job.

Even worse than the smell and the dead bodies and the middle-of-the-night summonings was the fact that all their watching and waiting and hoping was usually for naught.

To be fair, there was a well-publicized account of a watchman who found a presumed-dead five-year-old to be alive and well and playing with some white flowers. How exciting that must have been! Sure, it was unfortunate that the child's grieving mother—upon hearing the miraculous news that her kid was alive—became so overcome with joy that she died herself. But nonetheless, a child had been saved!

Or maybe not.

Because the story ended up being a huge fake.

Also apparently bogus? The report that ten presumed-dead people had woken in a waiting mortuary in Berlin over a period of two and a half years.

In the end, it isn't clear if anyone, ever, was saved by a waiting mortuary.

Q: What did the man say after he was almost buried alive?

A: Phew! *That* was almost a grave mistake!

Chapter 6

When Maggots Tell Time

Job: Forensic Entomologist
Time Period: Now

Beatrice the blow fly's iridescent body shimmers in the sunlight as she flies over the riverbank. Her antennae are on full alert as they sniff the air. Finally, she gets a whiff of what she's been looking for: the scent of death.

She zooms off, following the smell. Upon arrival it's clear she's hit the jackpot—the animal has only been dead a matter of minutes. The body is that of one of those big, lumbering creatures. The kind that stomps around on two feet while making an obnoxious amount of noise. A human, she thinks they're called.

Beatrice does a quick flyover before landing on the human's face. She crawls into the gaping mouth. The ears. The cave-like nostrils.

The nostrils are perfect! Cozy. Moist. Dark. So Beatrice starts laying egg after egg after whitish-yellow egg.

Before long, Beatrice is surrounded by other blow flies. Like Bertha and Bernadette. Blanche and that show-off Bessie. And countless others who've been attracted by the death smell.

Soon the human's eyes, nose, mouth, and even the giant, cavernous wound on his stomach are packed with blow fly eggs.

Beatrice lays her last egg and takes to the air. "Good luck, my darlings," she whispers. "Good luck."

Okay, so blow flies don't actually whisper their well wishes to their eggs. And they probably don't go around calling themselves Bernadette or Bessie. But blow flies *do* have the remarkable ability to sniff out a body within minutes of death.

And thank goodness they do. These flies and the eggs they lay provide vital clues for forensic entomologists—the headliners of this chapter.

But we're getting a bit ahead of ourselves. Let's go back

to our body—the one Beatrice the blow fly was going gaga over. Beatrice may have found the body right away, but we humans don't have her super-sniffing antennae. Depending on where the body is located, it may take hours, days, weeks, even months before someone finds the corpse and calls 911.

Once the authorities are alerted, though, it won't be long before the area is overrun with detectives, evidence bags, police tape, and cameras. Dental records will hopefully soon determine the body's identity, but considering the man's gaping stomach wound, it appears he was murdered. The police have multiple questions they need to find answers to.

Like when the man died.

The answer to this question is critical, as it helps detectives narrow down a whodunit suspect list. If the man died while his wife was out of the country on business, she's got an alibi. But if he died hours after they were witnessed having a rip-roaring fight? Well . . . that's a different story.

Determining time of death can be tricky, but with the help of forensics (the use of science to investigate a crime), a good guess can usually be made. If a body hasn't been dead that long, a detective can look for several clues:

- **Body stiffness: Starting a couple of hours after death, a body's muscles get rigid. Hard. Inflexible. This lasts for about a day and a half before the muscles become soft again. But depending on the health of the person and what they were doing right before death, this stiffness occurs more quickly in some than in others. It's anything but exact.**

- Body temperature: In the hour after death, a body's temperature stays fairly constant—or even increases slightly—and then it slowly drifts down until it reaches the temperature of its surroundings. But lots of factors influence how fast a corpse cools after death; temperature doesn't tell everything.

- Skin appearance: As tissues run out of oxygen and gravity causes blood to pool, the color and appearance of the skin will change. These skin changes progress through specific stages after a person dies. But this also isn't perfect.

Because none of these techniques are absolute, researchers have tried to find a more reliable way to determine an exact time of death. They've even tried analyzing eyeball fluid! But despite all their efforts, we still have no foolproof, when-did-this-person-die clock for forensic experts to go by. So they need to put together *all* the clues—the body's stiffness, its temperature, its color—and make an educated guess. Usually they can get pretty close.

But what happens when a body is past the stage where these early clues are helpful? When the body has been dead for days? Or weeks? Or months? It might seem impossible.

But it's not.

Not if you have a good forensic entomologist to call upon, that is.

Entomologists are bug people. Like an Egyptologist is an expert on ancient Egypt and a scatologist is an expert on all things poop, an entomologist's realm is that of the insect world.

And a *forensic* entomologist is a person who uses bugs to solve crimes.

Flies on a Sickle

Considering that forensic entomology is in many ways a new profession, it's fascinating to learn that bugs were used to solve a crime way back in the thirteenth century. As depicted in the book *The Washing Away of Wrongs*, the Chinese official Sung Tz'u tells the story of a man who was found dead along a road. A death investigator was called to the scene and determined that the man had been slashed to death using a sharp, curved farming tool called a sickle.

Unfortunately, sickles were everywhere in the Chinese village where the man had lived. Anyone who was anyone had one.

So whose sickle had done the slashing?

After the victim's wife and neighbors were interviewed, the crime remained unsolved. The death investigator therefore switched tactics and asked everyone in the village to come together at an appointed time, sickle in hand. Before long, the investigator had seventy or eighty sickles lying in front of him on the ground.

The sickles looked practically identical to the people hovering around. There was nothing to make one sickle stand out among the others. Thankfully, however, the sickles looked very different to the gathering flies. They were immediately drawn to one sickle out of the bunch.

Knowing that flies are attracted to blood and rotting flesh, the investigator accused that sickle's owner of being the murderer. In the face of the buzzing evidence, the man confessed.

Bugs like Beatrice the blow fly—the dead body–sniffing equivalent to a drug-sniffing dog.

As we've already learned, Beatrice and her blow fly friends don't come to the body just to slurp up some blood or saliva. They also come to find a cozy, dark, moist place to serve as the perfect baby-fly nursery. And because thousands of flies can swarm a body, each one laying hundreds of eggs, it doesn't take long before the body makes the Easter Bunny's egg-decorating workshop look like a joke.

Within about twenty-four hours of being laid, those eggs start to hatch and out crawl thousands and thousands of larvae—otherwise known as maggots. Over the following days, the maggots will chow down on the surrounding human flesh as they progress through three stages of life, called instars. The main difference between these three stages is size, as the wiggly, white maggots go from being two millimeters long to eight-ish millimeters long to about two centimeters long.

After days of stuffing themselves on the all-you-can-eat corpse buffet, the larvae crawl away to find a nice, dry spot to hide. Once hidden, their thin maggoty skin transforms into a thicker brown pupal casing that will shelter the larvae as they begin their ultimate transformation. After about a week or so, a *fly* will miraculously emerge from the casing, just as a butterfly emerges from a cocoon.

If the fly happens to be a female, before too long she'll be ready to lay eggs of her own. And thus the cycle begins again.

This predictable blow fly life cycle—from egg to little maggot to bigger maggot to bigger-yet maggot to pupa to fly—is exceedingly helpful to forensic entomologists. Depending on what stages of blow fly are found on or near a body, the entomologist can estimate how long ago the blow flies found the corpse. For example, if they find empty pupa casings by some human remains, they can be fairly sure the body died at least two weeks before. If all they find are eggs, the body is clearly quite fresh.

Unfortunately, even though blow fly eggs always go through the same stages in the same order, the speed with which they progress through these stages is weather dependent. The warmer it is, the faster blow flies mature. And if temperatures dip below 52 degrees Fahrenheit, blow flies go dormant until it warms up again. So forensic entomologists always need to consider recent weather conditions when making their determinations.

And for those times when the weather makes things difficult, it's lucky that forensic entomologists don't have to depend completely on blow flies. A dead body is a virtual arthropod zoo, and because each bug tends to show up on a corpse at a fairly specific time, they can all tell a story.

Large wasp species arrive quickly after a body dies. Their main targets are the blow flies themselves. Ants show up to eat the fly eggs and maggots. Tiny, can-be-less-than-one-millimeter wasps come slightly later to lay their own eggs. But they don't lay them on the body itself. Nope. Their victims are the maggots. When these wasp eggs hatch, hundreds of baby wasps can burst out of a single maggot! Tons of beetles, mites, and spiders also come by the body to check things out.

As forensic entomologists study these insects, they can often get further clues as to the time of death. Some insects, for instance, lay eggs only during specific times of the year. So if a body is found during the winter but it shows evidence of insect activity from a species that exclusively lays eggs

A Maggot's Mother

The fly life cycle, from egg to maggot to pupa to fly, is well known nowadays. When we see a bunch of wiggling maggots, we know they're there thanks to some insect eggs. But where did people living hundreds and thousands of years ago think maggots came from?

From spontaneous generation. Instead of having a mom and a dad, they simply . . . appeared. Having been created by the meat itself.

It's easy to see why people believed this. Leave some meat on a counter overnight and in a day or two it would be crawling with maggots. Nobody ever saw a mommy maggot or a daddy maggot. And who would think to connect the maggots to flies? They look nothing alike.

BUT LOOK! ALL THAT MEAT, JUST OVER THERE!

THE ROT IS ALWAYS GREENER ON THE OTHER CORPSE.

It was in the 1660s that Italian scientist Francesco Redi started suspecting the truth. To test things out, he put meat in several jars. Some jars he covered with mesh to keep flies out. Others he left open.

Then he waited.

All the meat started to get rotten, but maggots exclusively appeared on the meat in the open jars.

Redi repeated this experiment multiple times using all kinds of different meats, but no matter what he did, the outcome was the same. Meat only became maggoty if it was exposed to flies.

Maggot Feeding Frenzies

Considering how tiny maggots are, they're incredible eating machines. Sure, they have a mouth hook they can use to tear into flesh, but even with this it's hard to imagine how a bunch of minuscule, squishy, wiggly things can eat a dead body. They don't even have teeth!

Turns out maggots are such good eating machines because they do things differently than we do. As humans, we break down food *inside* our bodies. We chew everything into little pieces with our teeth and let the enzymes in our saliva and stomachs do the rest.

Maggots, on the other hand, don't keep their enzymes inside. They secrete them into the outside world to do all the digesting out there. Then the maggots glide through the broken-down mush and gulp it up.

Can the enzymes from one little maggot really do that much digesting, though? Truthfully, no. But when a female blow fly lays her hundreds of eggs, those eggs often hatch within *minutes* of each other. And female flies like to lay their eggs where other flies are laying eggs. End result: When the eggs hatch, thousands of maggots end up swarming together in a huge, writhing mass. And the combined digestive enzymes of the entire maggot heap? Well, they can do an awful lot of damage.

during the spring, they know the body has been there at least since spring.

All things considered, a forensic entomologist will not be able to use bug evidence to tell detectives *exactly* when a person died. But by using their bug smarts, they can greatly narrow down the how-old-is-this-body window. Which is amazing! And—to those of us who get the heebie-jeebies at the mere thought of plucking a wiggling maggot out of the nostril of a bloated dead body—also very gross!

Q: Why was the forensic entomologist irritated by the insects he was studying?

A: They kept bugging him!

Insects Tell All

When forensic entomologists study the flies and maggots and other body-munching critters on a corpse, their main goal is usually to determine time of death. But studying insects can provide investigators with other clues as well.

Some species only live at certain elevations or in certain climates. Some prefer urban environments and others rural. In certain situations, this information can be extremely helpful. For example, if a body is found in the middle of the woods but the maggots plucked out of its eye sockets belong to a fly species that exclusively lives in cities, the person most likely died in the city. And was dumped in the country.

Insects can also help detectives locate injuries. Flies enjoy laying their eggs in natural openings (think nose, eyes, mouth, ears) and in bloody wounds. So if there is a mass of happy maggots feasting away in a body's chest, whereas most of the body has thus far been untouched, chances are there was an injury there. This can help detectives determine cause of death.

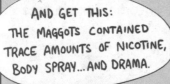

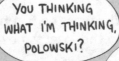

Maggots can also tell if a person had drugs in their system. Maggots that chow down on a person who recently used cocaine, for example, will contain cocaine.

So even though maggots cannot speak, they can still tell us a whole lot.

The Body Farm

The Body Farm. There is no doubt those words sound a bit grizzly. Like the title of a bad horror movie. But what is it really?

The Body Farm, also known by its more official title of the Anthropology Research Facility, is located in Knoxville, Tennessee. The brainchild of Dr. William Bass, the Body Farm is a place where human corpses are laid out and left to rot.

That's right. To rot.

And while the bodies rot away, they are carefully scrutinized. The whole point is to determine how human bodies decompose under various conditions. Like how soon do maggots appear on a body if it's left out in 70-degree sunny weather versus a chilly fall day? How fast does a body break down if it is naked? Or clothed? Or wrapped in plastic? And what if it's buried three feet underground or left in the trunk of a car?

The whole Body Farm thing might sound strange, but the observations made there can help detectives solve crimes.

And believe it or not, approximately one hundred bodies are donated to the Body Farm *every year*!

Chapter 7

Bedpan, Anyone?

Job: Nursing Assistant

Time Period: Now

In chapter 3, we learned all about the barber-surgeons of the Middle Ages. We saw how they dealt with pus-filled boils and rotten teeth. How they chopped off limbs, stuck needles into eyeballs, and plucked out head lice.

Well, thanks to better hygiene, better anesthesia, and better medical knowledge, a trip to a health-care facility nowadays is light-years away from what a trip to a barber-surgeon's office would have been like a thousand years ago. But let's not fool ourselves. This doesn't mean the medical world is no longer disgusting. No siree! It's still jam-packed with sights and smells that would make your stomach roil. Big time.

To ease our way into this health-care grossness a bit, let's start out in my own clinic. As a doctor, I specialized in allergies and asthma. And some allergies, like those to cats and pollen and dust mite poo, can really mess with a person's nose—effectively turning it into a stuffy, sneezy snot factory. Given all this, my physical exam obviously had to include a quick peek up the schnoz.

My tool for this task: an otoscope (or, as I more commonly called it, a nose-looker-inner). The otoscope—with a disposable tip on it, of course!—got shoved right up the patient's nostril.

I referred to this part of the exam as a "booger check," but this nose exploration was about a whole lot more than checking out the snot. It was also a way to see how stuffy things were. To evaluate the color of the nasal tissues. To look for any unwanted growths—called polyps. And to make sure there were no Perler beads, Skittles, or Lego-man heads hanging out up there causing problems.

Not surprisingly, my kid patients were often appalled by this nose part of the exam. They couldn't imagine anything worse than looking at boogers all day long. My response: It could be worse.

Way worse.

Some doctors, called urologists, focus on the urinary tract. In simplistic terms, if it's a part of the body that touches pee, a urologist specializes in it.

There are gastroenterologists who deal with the gut. They take care of patients with constipation. Bloody vomit. Mucusy diarrhea. These docs stick long, snakelike cameras down people's throats and up their you-know-whats.

Pathologists spend much of their doctoring time looking at human tissues under a microscope, but some of them also do autopsies. This means they cut up dead bodies and examine every nook and cranny in an attempt to uncover the cause of death.

And last but not least, there are proctologists. These doctors specialize in the rectum and anus. They look at buttholes all day long.

Considering these alternatives, I say bring on the snotty noses!

Medical doctors are also not alone in having icky tasks to do. Lots of other health-care jobs would make you shudder. Like phlebotomists. These modern-day bloodletters stick needles into arms to draw blood. At least they don't have to use leeches to get their samples.

Or podiatrists, who are medical professionals who specialize in the feet. Even the stinky, warty, infected ones!

There are wound care nurses who spend their days taking care of oozing sores.

Shepherd of the Anus

In ancient Egypt, during the days of the pharaohs, medicine was a little different from what it is today. Wait. Scratch that. It was *a lot* different. Have a bleeding wound? Stick some raw meat on it. Have a cold? All you need is an incantation . . . and the milk of a woman who gave birth to a boy.

Like today, though, the ancient Egyptian medical professionals could focus their attention on one specific area of the body if they wanted. They had specialists focusing on the eyes and specialists focusing on the teeth. There were those who dealt with the head. And those in charge of the butt.

What were those butt experts called?

They were called guardians of the anus! Or—depending on the translator—shepherds of the anus.

There are the cleaning staff, who deal with the monstrous messes left behind by sick patients and messy physicians.

And then there are the nursing assistants, who definitely earn my vote for grossest job in health care today. On the surface, their job description doesn't sound all that bad. They help patients with simple, everyday activities.

Battlefield Beginnings

As unexpected as this might sound, the job of nursing assistant—at least in the United States—had its beginning in war. During World War I, nurses were swamped. As hard as they tried, they couldn't keep up with the workload. There were simply too many wounded soldiers to care for.

So in 1918, the Red Cross founded the Volunteer Nurses' Aide Service to provide the nurses with assistants. These aides did all the straightforward tasks, which allowed the nurses to focus on the big stuff.

The end result was that nurses now had some much-needed help. And the career of nursing assistant was born.

But let's consider *your* daily routine for a minute to see how quickly "helping with daily activities" can veer into where-is-the-nearest-puke-bucket territory.

When you wake up in the morning, what do you do first? Maybe you vamoose your dragon-killing morning breath with your fancy-schmancy electric toothbrush and some minty toothpaste. Well, if a patient can't brush on their own, a nursing assistant comes to the rescue. They brave the stench to get the job done.

Next, you might go to the bathroom. You probably make your way to the toilet and get situated on top without any help, but not all patients can do this. A nursing assistant might have to help them onto the toilet or get them settled on a bedpan. And if the patient calls for help a second too late or if the bathroom ends up being a few steps too far, watch out!

Next up? You wipe your derriere to remove all the poop and pee, right? Well, in hospitals and nursing homes, these toilet paper responsibilities are often delegated to a nursing assistant.

Pooping done, it's time to do some hair grooming. So a nursing assistant might grab a brush to tame the unruly bedhead. Or trim a beard that *hopefully* doesn't have any remnants of last night's spaghetti dinner lurking between the hairs.

On bath days, a nursing assistant will gather up some soap and a sponge and get scrubbing. Ideally it'll only be dirt

Magicking Away Morning Breath

What are the five worst things you've ever smelled? Vomit? The spray of a skunk? Your grandma's farts? That leftover tuna-fish salad your brother stuck in the fridge and then forgot about for a month?

Or what about your dad's morning breath? You've got to admit, that's pretty stinky.

Thinking of morning breath, it's hard not to feel sorry for the nursing assistants who have to come face-to-face with foul-smelling caves of chompers every morning. But on the bright side, at least they have good tools to work with. Tools like toothbrushes, toothpaste, and maybe even some germ-killing mouthwash.

But what did halitosis (bad breath) sufferers do before modern toothpaste was introduced to the world in the nineteenth century? Did their morning breath turn into all-day breath?

While there *were* a whole lot of very smelly mouths in antiquity, this didn't mean that nobody tried to sweeten things up. Many people chewed on pleasant-smelling herbs and spices to mask the bad smells. In ancient Egypt, they made breath mints out of honey, frankincense, myrrh, and cinnamon. During the Ming Dynasty in China, a toothbrush was invented that used hog hairs as the bristles.

And then there was ancient Rome, where the Roman citizens took a much more off-putting approach to their bad breath problem. According to historian Pliny the Elder, they rubbed their teeth with honey.

And the ashes of burnt mouse droppings!

and sweat and sloughed-off dead skin cells that the nursing assistant will be washing off, but who are we kidding? When a patient is hospitalized with vomiting and diarrhea, you *know* the nursing assistant is cleaning off more than just yesterday's deodorant.

And if that's not enough, depending on where they work, a lucky nursing assistant might also get to bandage up seeping leg ulcers. Wipe the random poop dribble off the floor. And administer medications to the occasional less-than-willing patient.

All told, a nursing assistant clearly has a job full of unpleasant smells. Full of unpleasant sights. Full of unpleasant everythings.

But you know what? The job of nursing assistant isn't all bad.

And no. It's not the paycheck that redeems the job. According to the United States Bureau of Labor Statistics, in 2021 the median nursing assistant pay was a measly $14.56 an hour. This might sound like a fortune compared to your weekly allowance, but the median hourly pay for an elevator repairman that year was $47.05! And while I'm sure those elevator repairman earned every penny they got, unless they were having a very unfortunate day, at least they didn't need to deal with bloody vomit or did-something-die-in-there morning breath.

But if the pay doesn't redeem a nursing assistant's job, what does? Well, it turns out that patients in hospitals and nursing homes often come to love their nursing assistant even more than their doctors or nurses. And possibly even more than their five-hour-long naps, their jigsaw puzzles, and their knitting. Why is this? It's because a nursing assistant spends a whole lot of one-on-one time with their patients. While helping an old man to the toilet or shampooing a hospitalized child's hair, a nursing assistant can ask questions. Tell jokes. Chat. Listen. And just be there.

So ultimately a nursing assistant has an undeniably stomach-churning job, but they also make their patients' lives significantly better. I think we can all give three cheers for nursing assistants!

Q: Why did the nursing assistant go to art school?

A: To learn how to draw blood.

Attention! Attention! Butt Wipers Across the Country Work Without Pay

Some of the tasks that nursing assistants are called upon to do might sound awful, but did you know there are *unpaid* people out in the world who are daily called upon to do similar jobs? They wipe butts. They clean up puke. They sacrifice their sleep to care for others. And not only do they not get paid, much of the time they don't even get a "thank you" for their troubles.

What ridiculous person would agree to such a job?

A parent.

PART 2

THE GROSSEST JOBS DEALING WITH POOP, PEE, AND VOMIT

Chapter 8

It's a Puke Party!

Job: Dining Room Attendant
Time Period: Ancient Rome

Time to play make-believe. Let's pretend you don't live in the twenty-first century anymore. It's bye-bye chocolate milkshakes. Bye-bye NFL football. Bye-bye comfortable underwear. Your new home for the foreseeable future: ancient Rome. The land of Julius Caesar, temples, gladiator battles, and togas.

Right now I suspect you're worried that I'll make you be a dining room attendant—this chapter's vomit-inducing job. But lucky for you, I'm in a good mood today. So not only will I save you from *that* fate, I'll also let you be rich!

Nice of me, huh?

The only problem is, now that you're an ancient Roman with loads of cash, you need to find a way to spend your fortune. Maybe you can purchase a nice getaway home in the country. Donate huge sums of dough to build a new bathhouse in the center of town. Buy an extra-fancy chamber pot to do your business in.

Or perhaps you'd like to throw a dinner party.

Because dinner parties in ancient Rome? They're all the rage.

And just to be clear, when I say "dinner party," I'm not talking about some last-minute, let's-get-takeout-and-watch-Netflix-all-night-type thing. Also out? Potlucks. Make-your-own-pizza parties. And picnics by the lake where everyone sits crisscross applesauce on a flannel blanket.

Rather, I'm talking about a super-fancy, show-off-your-wealth, hobnob-with-the-bigwigs party.

I know, I know. An event like that sounds frightfully boring to me, too. But the ancient Romans sure loved them.

To throw a successful party, there are lots of things you

must figure out. Like the menu. It needs to be unique. Expensive. Memorable. Sure, it can contain *some* mundane foodstuffs, like fruit and veggies and pig udders and chicken, but if your goal is to make an impression—which, let's be honest, is the number one goal of any ancient Roman dinner party—you can't stop there. You need something more. Like ostrich. Or peacock brains. Or flamingo tongue.

Nothing Like a Little Belch to Say "Delicious!"

Have you ever burped at the dinner table? What happened? Your little brother laughed until milk squirted out of his nose, didn't he? And I bet your older sister tried to one-up you. (She is a pretty good belcher, after all.) And your mom? Oh man. If looks could kill.

But if you lived in ancient Rome, your mom probably wouldn't have been bothered by your little expulsion of mouth air. Why is this? Because many people believe the ancient Romans belched as a way of showing their appreciation for a good meal!

BLEURGHH

You also need to arrange some entertainment to keep your guests amused while they eat. How about some music? A poetry reading? Or you can hire dancers, acrobats, actors, or wrestlers to put on a show.

Menu planned. Entertainment figured out. Now you need your guest list. Assuming you want to follow normal ancient Roman operating procedure, you want to end up with exactly nine diners. Please make sure at least one of them is a major VIP. They'll make your party seem extra important.

Next, you need the right furniture. You can't just have everyone sit around a table in a bunch of straight-backed wooden chairs, and we've already ruled out a blanket by the lake. No, what you want are couches.

Yup. Couches.

Your guests will eat their dinner lying down, propped up on their left elbow. This may sound kind of nice—like eating dinner while lounging in front of the TV—but there's a twist. The ancient Romans use *three-person* couches. As in three different people lie squashed together on a single couch! So much for elbow room. Because you'll have nine diners, you should get three couches. Arrange them in a U-shaped pattern around the table.

So at this point, you have your couches. Your menu. Your entertainment. Your guest list. Next up: your seating chart (or, if we want to be more precise, your *lying* chart). If your plan up till now had been to simply let your guests sprawl out wherever the heck they want, don't! That isn't how things work.

No Dirty Diners Allowed!

As a transported-back-in-time Roman citizen, there is something you'll probably come to love just as much as a fancy dinner party: a good bath. You may spend hour after hour at a bathhouse.

Every day!

A trip to a bathhouse sounds simple, but it's actually quite an ordeal. Definitely more involved than soaking in a fancy whirlpool tub until your fingers look like raisins.

As you might guess, there is an element of getting clean involved, although you won't immediately recognize what the ancient Romans do as "cleaning." First, oil is rubbed all over your body. Then a curved tool, called a strigil, is used to scrape off the oil and any dirt, sweat, or dead skin cells that come with it. It sounds wacky, but it does the job well enough.

A bathhouse excursion also entails—surprise, surprise—spending time in the water. You can swim laps, relax, gossip, or even conduct a business deal or two while soaking in your choice of hot or cold pools. Because ancient Romans don't wear swimming suits, you'll be swimming laps, relaxing, gossiping, and conducting business deals while in the buff.

Most bathhouses also contain gyms for exercising and lifting weights. You can get a massage. If you're running on empty, you'll find restaurants and snack bars. And if the bathhouse is large enough, you may even find a theater. A library. A garden for strolling. Even a gift shop.

Sure sounds like a very nice way to spend an afternoon,

doesn't it? And thanks to the popularity of bathhouses, there is an extra bonus. Whenever you throw a dinner party, you can rest assured that your guests will arrive squeaky clean. The aroma of eel eggs—and not the smell of a Roman with a bad case of BO—will be front and center.

There has to be a specific spot for each person. A spot for the host. A spot for the most important guest. A spot for the second-most-important guest. And on and on down the line. It's something like ranking your school friends from favorite to second favorite to . . . not so favorite.

And now, finally, after all that planning, it's time for your party! Your guests will arrive, everyone will lie down on their assigned couch, the food will be served, and as your guests start chowing down all around you, please do not waste a single anxious second agonizing over which fork is the salad fork or which fork is the fish fork. Because it doesn't matter.

Ancient Romans didn't typically use forks at their fancy dinner parties. And they often didn't even use spoons.

They ate with their hands!

Some of them ate neatly, even when using their paws as utensils. But if the art of the time period is to be trusted, this was often not the case. Instead of placing table scraps in tidy piles, many Romans took their fish tails, snail shells, and I-don't-like-this-exotic-dish-very-much-after-all food chunks and tossed them. Right onto the floor.

Also tossed? Their cookies.

And no. The cookies being tossed were not of the oatmeal raisin or chocolate chip variety. When your guests toss their cookies, what they're actually doing is throwing up. Hurling. Blowing chunks. In the words of the ancient Roman philosopher Seneca, "The Romans vomit that they may eat, and eat that they may vomit."

Now, it has to be said that most Romans *did not* go around vomiting on the floor at dinner parties. But some did. I mean, what else is a person whose stomach is stuffed full of dormice and fish livers supposed to do when a platter of heavily spiced flamingo tongues appears in front of them? By spewing everything up, they had room for more.

The Famous Vomitorium

If you've read much about ancient Rome, chances are you've come across the word "vomitorium." You probably learned that it was a room designed specifically for overstuffed Romans to puke in.

While having a designated hurling room does sound better than having people vomit onto the dining room floor, it also sounds a bit far-fetched.

And far-fetched it was, because there was no such thing!

So what was a vomitorium if it wasn't a puke chamber? It was the most boring of places: the part of a theater or amphitheater that people walk through when entering from or exiting to the street.

As a transported-back-in-time ancient Roman, watching your floor become blanketed with lobster tails and puke puddles will undoubtedly make you start worrying about one thing: Who will be assigned cleanup duty? Because we all know what your current-day mom would do if you threw a party like that. You'd be on your hands and knees with a rag

How About a Doggie Bag?

These days, the host of a dinner party will sometimes send extra food home with their guests. After all, who needs five pounds of sliced ham, two trays of veggies, or fifteen pieces of cake sitting around? But this isn't an expectation. At all. Most guests will go home with a full tummy and be satisfied.

In ancient Rome, however, things were different. Guests *expected* to go home from a party with extra food. That way they didn't only get pig udders and bird brains at the party. They'd get to enjoy them all over again the next day. As leftovers!

and a bucket of soapy water faster than you can say, "Great. I've been grounded for life."

But in ancient Rome, the people throwing the party didn't do the cleaning. The guests didn't do the cleaning. It wasn't even the host's children who did the cleaning.

It was way worse than that.

You see, in ancient Rome, not all people were free. Many were enslaved. And it was the enslaved people "owned" by the wealthy Roman hosting the dinner party who got the horrible, disgusting, demeaning job of dining room attendant. *They* were the ones cleaning up the mess.

Actually, enslaved people were not only called upon at the end of the meal to deal with the vomit splatters and food scraps. They had more on their plates than just getting the floor and table and couches squeaky clean and ready for the next dinner party.

Enslaved people were also the ones laboring away in the hot kitchen. They made the stuffed dormice and fermented fish sauce and eel eggs that eventually wound up in the guests' stomachs and scattered across the ground. They were the ones who served the food. Who washed the guests' hands between courses. Who held out containers in hopes of catching some of the puke *before* it made its way onto the floor. And if they were good musicians or speakers or dancers, they might have been called upon to be the entertainment.

In the end, it's clear. You should be thanking me profusely

for sending you back in time as a free, rich Roman. Because you sure wouldn't want to wind up a dining room attendant at a fancy dinner party!

Q: Why did the guest decide to leave the ancient Roman dinner party?

A: Because something came up! Blargh!

Ancient Rome's Dirty Little Secret

Picture ancient Rome and it's hard not to envision the Roman Colosseum, the Pantheon, the massive arches. But if you thought all those architectural masterpieces were built by happy, free, well-paid Romans, think again. Most of the hard, dirty work done throughout ancient Rome wasn't done by Roman citizens at all; it was done by enslaved people.

People could find themselves enslaved for multiple reasons. Sometimes they were former citizens of a land the Roman Empire had conquered. Some Roman citizens became enslaved because they were so far in debt they had no hope of ever repaying their loans. Children were sometimes sold into slavery *by their own parents* because the family was too poor to feed them.

Depending on what skills an enslaved person possessed,

they could be called upon to perform a whole host of different tasks. They might work as a doctor. A tutor. A hairdresser. A dining room attendant.

They could be used to build bridges, aqueducts, temples, and bathhouses. They might be sent to the mines to do dangerous, backbreaking work until it killed them.

Or they might end up at a gladiator school. Which essentially guaranteed them a bloody, painful, not-too-far-in-the-future death.

It's a horrendously sad reality, but many of the incredible things ancient Rome is known for were only possible because of the hard, thankless work of enslaved people.

Chapter 9

My, What a Beautiful Toga You Have!

Job: Fuller

Time Period: From Ancient Rome
Through the Middle Ages and Beyond

Let's face it: Some people care a lot about their clothes; others couldn't care less. Maybe you follow each and every fashion trend, whatever it may be. Or perhaps you use your wardrobe—with your impressive collection of hedgehog socks and avocado bowties—to show off your uniqueness. Or then again, maybe your innermost wish is that every day could be PJ day.

But regardless of how much or how little you care about the fashion world, at a minimum you probably want two things: You want your clothes to be fairly clean and not too uncomfortable. No bright red splotches of spaghetti sauce decorating your vintage T-shirt. No frilly dresses made out of some coarse, prickly, makes-you-want-to-scratch-your-skin-off fabric. And absolutely, positively no yellow armpit stains.

This desire to have clean and comfortable clothes is nothing new. People living in ancient Rome also wanted this. And it was the disgusting job of the fuller to give the people what they wanted.

The fabric of choice at that time was wool, a material that technically could come from all kinds of animals. Like goats and alpacas. Llamas and camels. Even some rabbits. But in ancient Rome, it was sheep wool that ruled the day.

Now if you've ever seen a sheep in real life, you probably thought it looked fluffy. Like the sheep was covered in cotton balls or, if you were feeling peckish at the time, cotton candy. But in reality, wool is coarse. Greasy. And downright filthy.

All things considered, the greasy and filthy part isn't that surprising. Sheep usually go a full year between shearings (i.e., haircuts), and during that year their options for getting clean are pretty limited. The nearest Roman bathhouse or YMCA pool or inflatable backyard kiddie pool is bound to have a strict no-sheep policy. Which means the closest a sheep can get to a good wash is standing outside in the rain.

It's therefore no wonder that after an ancient Roman sheared their sheep, the first thing they did was give the wool a quick rinse to get rid of at least some of the gunk. Then the sheep fuzz may or may not have been dyed before it was spun into yarn. And then woven into cloth.

Now at this point you might think the ancient Roman tailors would be all good to go, seeing that they had fabric and everything. But no. That initial cloth was anything but toga-worthy. No self-respecting Roman would wear it. Not only was the material still too greasy and dirty, but the strands of wool had not yet come together. There were gaps between the fibers, like what you'd get if you weaved together a bunch of dried dandelion stems.

Luckily for the toga-wearing Romans, though, there were fullers around to turn that mess of a cloth into something even the most dignified Roman would be pleased with. A fuller simply needed to do three things to the wool: clean it, degrease it, and force the individual strands to come together.

When it came to cleaning, it was a bad break for the fuller that he couldn't simply buy some lavender-scented laundry detergent at the local big-box store. Because there were no sudsy laundry detergents at the time. Or big-box stores, for that matter.

The fuller was therefore stuck using a much more revolting cleaner: urine.

Or *stale* urine to be exact.

To our twenty-first–century ears, using pee as a cleaner sounds beyond ridiculous. If you've ever had an accident in the middle of science class, your first thought undoubtedly wasn't "Awesome! Now I don't need to wash these jeans tonight!"

But if we allowed our pee to sit around and get stale like

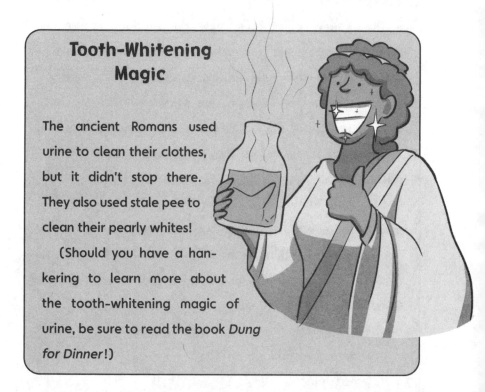

Tooth-Whitening Magic

The ancient Romans used urine to clean their clothes, but it didn't stop there. They also used stale pee to clean their pearly whites!

(Should you have a hankering to learn more about the tooth-whitening magic of urine, be sure to read the book *Dung for Dinner*!)

the ancient Romans did, well, presto chango! It would gain some useful properties.

This is because when pee comes out of a person—or a

Filling the Fuller's Pee Pots

I'm sure you've been wondering where the ancient Roman fuller got his pee. Well . . . we don't know for sure. Some likely came from the fuller's own bladder. Some could have come from the public lavatory down the street. And many historians believe fullers got much of their urine from pee pots placed throughout the Roman empire for full-bladdered Romans to use.

Then again, considering how our modern-day recycling bins often get misused—what with all the trash and other junk that gets carelessly tossed in—it's hard to imagine the ancient Roman pee pots would be treated any better. And since fullers used the urine to *clean* with, it seems they'd want more pristine stock.

But who knows. The ancient Romans may have been much better than we are about putting everything away. Trash in the garbage can. Urine in the pee pots. Vomit on the dining room floor.

You know. Everything in its proper place.

dog, an aardvark, or a wombat—it's full of something called urea. Given a little time, that urea breaks down into ammonia and bicarbonate. And that ammonia? It's a super-duper cleaner!

So now we know the fuller used pee to clean his wool, but how did he deal with the grease part? Conveniently, the stale urine helped with this as well. As the urea in the urine was making its fancy transformation into ammonia and bicarbonate, the urine became alkaline. And alkaline solutions are great at dissolving fats and oils—like the grease found in sheep wool.

Thanks to pee, the fuller could now clean and degrease cloth. But he still needed to force the wool fibers to come together. He needed to close up the gaps and make the fabric smooth, thick, and strong. Well, fortunately for the fuller, and for all wool enthusiasts out there, wool fibers love to join together. It just takes a bit of heat, moisture, and pressure to prod them along.

The fuller would undoubtedly have loved to use a washing machine to provide the heat, moisture, and pressure for him. To toss in some cloth, pour in a cup or two of stale urine, push the "eco-cycle" button, and sit back and sip away at a vanilla latte while the machine did all the work. But the first electric washing machine arrived in the world in the twentieth century. The fuller of ancient Rome was a couple thousand years too early.

Instead, the fuller had to use a more hands-on approach. Or, rather, a more feet-on approach. Because the tool he used?

Was his very own tootsies.

Here's what he did. He'd place the wool cloth in a large vat and dump in some stale pee, often along with a grease-absorbing clay called fuller's earth. He'd yank up his toga, hop on in, and start stomping. He'd stomp and stomp and stomp on that single piece of cloth. For hours!

The pressure and heat generated from the clomping caused the wool strands to bind together while the urine did the cleaning and degreasing. It was a stinky, detestable win-win-win.

Stomping away on some pee-soaked cloth wasn't tricky, but knowing when to stop stomping was. If a fuller stopped too soon, the wool would still be greasy and dirty. The strands wouldn't have come together enough. But stomp too much in one area of the cloth and the wool would become thin, even holey. The cloth would be ruined and the poor fuller would have to begin the whole mind-numbingly boring process all over again with some brand-new cloth and some new (old) pee.

If the fuller got things right, though, the masterpiece was dried, and then a brush—made from thistles or hedgehog skin—was used to remove any lint. To finish everything off, the cloth might be spread over a pot of burning sulfur to bleach it, or it could be rubbed with fuller's earth to bring out the color.

Once the wool was deemed ready, it was turned into something fabulous. Like a brand-new toga for Julius Caesar.

But what if that perfect, clean, degreased toga got puked

on during an ancient Roman dinner party? No worries. The toga's owner simply hauled it back to the fuller, who'd use some stale urine to get it clean again. Like the ancient Rome version of a dry cleaner.

Taxing the Yellow Stuff

Taxes. They're used to pay for some super-important stuff—like fixing potholes, funding public schools, and paying for lifesaving research. But that doesn't keep most adults from complaining about paying them.

Especially because we need to deal with so many forms of taxes. Like property tax. Income tax. Sales tax. Urine tax.

Wait. What? A urine tax?

Nowadays urine is one thing we are thankfully *not* taxed on. But if you lived in ancient Rome during the time of Emperor Vespasian, a urine tax was a real thing! It was a tax most likely paid by professionals who—like our trusty pee-stomping fullers—needed to get their hands on lots of the yellow stuff to do their daily work.

WOMEN   MEN

Considering how icky the whole pee-cleaning thing sounds, one would hope that as ancient Rome became ancient history, humans would have left it behind.

But no. Pee was still being used to clean and whiten cloth in colonial America!

Q: What did the fuller say to his son on Bring Your Child to Work Day?
A: Urine for a real treat!

My, What Luxurious Sheep Grease You Have

To protect their wool and skin from rain, harsh sunlight, and other rough weather conditions, sheep produce an oily, waxy secretion called lanolin. And lanolin—while still on the sheep—is a good thing.

Once the wool is off the sheep, however, the lanolin has got to go. Nobody wants a greasy wool sweater. That's just gross.

In ancient Rome, the fullers stomped in pee and fuller's earth to get rid of the lanolin. Nowadays, we remove the lanolin and add it to all kinds of products we put on our skin. Products like moisturizers and sunscreens and hemorrhoid creams and lipsticks.

In fact, it's possible you smeared some sheep grease on your face this very morning. Hopefully that thought doesn't make you want to baaaaa-rf!

DERMATOLOGIST APPROVED
SHEGRI
100% NATURAL SHEEP GREASE

Chapter 10

A Cart o' Poop

Job: Gongfermor
Time Period: Middle Ages and Beyond

Humans poop. It's a simple fact of life.

And for those of us living in the United States during the twenty-first century, when we poop, our turds get flushed down a toilet, never to be thought of again.

But let's give up our smartphones and fuzzy socks for a moment, hop into a time machine, and travel back to Europe during the Middle Ages. Back to the time of castles and land-less peasants and knights on horseback. Back to the time of leech collectors and barber-surgeons. Back to a time when there was nothing even closely resembling a modern flush toilet.

Now, be honest . . . this lack of flush toilets has you feel-ing a bit anxious about the whole going-back-in-time thing, doesn't it? Well, don't worry. There is no need to panic. At least not too much. Because lucky for you, there were gong-fermors around to deal with all the poo.

Before we get too busy talking about gongfermors, though, let's pause for a moment to learn the answer to one very important question: Without flush toilets, where *would* you do your business?

One possibility—especially if you lived in the country—was to poop in something like an outhouse. Whenever nature called, you'd sneak outside, pull down your trousers, sit on a bench with a hole cut into it, and poo away. Your feces would drop through the hole and fall into whatever was below. If you were lucky, it was a stream the poop plopped into. The current would carry your waste away so you didn't need to waste a single second dealing with it. Your poop was now the concern of anyone downstream using the water for bathing or drinking.

If your outhouse wasn't built over water, your poop prob-ably fell into a big hole or a cesspit. Cesspits were huge, stinky, excrement-holding pits. Sometimes they were lined with wood, sometimes with stone. But regardless of what they were made of, cesspits were typically designed so the urine and liquid poo would seep through the cracks and leak into the ground. Only the solid material was left behind to fill up the pit.

Now, let's face it: Outhouses are all fine and dandy, but sometimes you wouldn't want to use one. Like when you had a bad case of the runs and the outhouse was waaaaay too far away. Or when it was −21 degrees Fahrenheit and no way, José, were you trudging out into that cold air to sit your bare butt on a frozen seat.

Not only that, but if you lived in town, you probably didn't have an outhouse to begin with.

So what then?

Quite possibly you'd use a chamber pot. Stored under your bed or hidden away in a corner, a chamber pot was the perfect portable toilet. Business done, you'd dump the waste outside. Ideally into your cesspit. Or the local waterway.

Chamber Pot Fun

Chamber pots might have been used in ancient Rome and the Middle Ages, but it didn't stop there. People commonly used them well into the twentieth century, and—in some areas of the world—they're still used today.

Considering chamber pots have been used for such a long time, it's not surprising that they weren't all the same. Some were made out of tin or porcelain or glass. Some were made out of pure gold.

Some chamber pots were simple and unadorned. Others could be considered beautiful, what with their elaborately decorated porcelain surfaces.

There were chamber pots with faces—like Napoleon's or Adolf Hitler's—painted on the bottom of the bowl. Nothing makes pooping more satisfying, after all, than pooping on your enemy's head.

And then there were some chamber pots that strove for the humorous. Like the chamber pot design that featured a huge, staring eye on the bottom. Often with the words "Use me well and keep me clean, and I will not tell what I have seen" written around the eye.

Many towns and cities also had public toilets. These were great pooping alternatives, provided they were well maintained. If they weren't kept up, though? Enter at your own risk. Once a man reportedly fell through the weak floor of a bathroom and drowned in the cesspit below! (If you're like me, this gruesome story leaves you with a burning question: Which is the worst way to go—being buried alive or drowning in a pit of human excrement?)

Getting back to our pooping-in-the-Middle-Ages exploration, what if you were one of the fortunate ones? What if you had spare cash on hand? Would you slog out to an outhouse, poo in a chamber pot, or scamper to the local public toilet?

Maybe.

Or maybe not.

It's possible you'd have your own indoor bathroom. You could do your thing in the comfort of your own house and have a pipe or chute transport everything into a cesspit located in your backyard or in your cellar. You'd be living the dream—assuming we don't dwell on the whole you-now-have-a-stinky-poop-pile-in-your-basement thing.

And finally, what if you won the jackpot and lived in a castle? Where would you poop then? Depending on the castle, your bathroom—which would have been called a garderobe—may have stuck partway out of the castle wall, like a wart protruding from a witch's nose. These partially outside-the-wall garderobes were something else. If you harbor a secret fear of falling into a toilet, they would not be the ideal pooping spot for you. Because inside these garderobes there would be a bench with a hole in it. And below that hole? Nothing but air. You'd poop in the hole, and your turds would fall.

Fall.

Fall.

Until they landed with a plop into a cesspit, a river, a poop pile, or the moat.

Not all garderobes stuck out of a castle, though. Some were built right into the thick castle walls or in one of the towers. A slanted chute would carry the poop slipping and sliding from the toilet to the outside world—again usually into a moat, river, or cesspit.

As you can see, while living in the Middle Ages, you'd have lots of pooping options. But as you probably noticed, there were a couple major problems with the system.

First, a lot of poop ended up in the waterways. This contaminated drinking water and made people sick. And if enough feces ended up in a particular stream or river, it could kill off the fish and other animals living there.

The other problem? If the feces weren't sent on a river cruise, they typically ended up in a cesspit or dung pile. Meaning there were heaps of poop just sitting around, smelling up the world. Clearly that poop needed to be taken away or it would keep piling up and piling up and piling up until . . .

Okay, let's not contemplate the "until" any further. Let's just say it *had* to be taken away.

Thankfully, there were poop-cleaning heroes laboring away during the Middle Ages—and for hundreds of years thereafter—who dealt with this pressing poop problem.

These heroes were called gongfermors (or gong farmers, gong scourers, or night soil men).

It was the gongfermor's job to jump into cesspits and moats to dig out the waste. He'd be knee-deep, waist-deep, even chest-deep in the stinky stuff. He'd spend his workdays filling bucket after bucket with poop, which he'd load onto his wagon.

Once full, a wagon might be driven to a designated poop-dumping spot outside the city walls. Or the entire stinky load could be sold to neighboring farmers, who'd spread the poo on their fields. Or—if we fast-forward to London several hundred years after the end of the Middle Ages—they might have taken their wagons to the aptly named Dung Wharf. From there it would be loaded onto barges and sent away to be used as fertilizer.

Not surprisingly, a gongfermor worked the night shift. Nobody wanted to see him in action as he waded around in cesspits. And the last thing you wanted passing you on the street as you were buying roast beef in the market was a poop-laden gongfermor's wagon.

A gongfermor was also often forced to live outside the city walls. Because he smelled like you-know-what.

And not only that, a gongfermor's job was dangerous. He was digging around in human poop, for goodness' sake, and we all know feces is chock-full of bacteria and germs and worms and other stuff that can make a person sick. Gongfermors also sometimes died of asphyxiation from the noxious fumes they had to breathe in.

One Man's Trash Is Another Man's Treasure

If you're getting bored with your current hobby, whether it's bird-watching, juggling, playing chess against old people in the park, or collecting belly button fuzz, here's an idea for you: take up amateur privy digging!

As a privy digger, you'll spend your free time digging through ancient cesspits and outhouses. Instead of getting rid of the poop, like a gongfermor, your goal will be to seek treasures hidden *within* the poo. Treasures like bottles, plates, marbles, and all the other stuff that—once upon a time—someone tossed out with the rest of their waste.

If this sounds like the perfect next hobby for you, there is one all-important rule you must follow. Make sure to always, always, always get permission from the landowners before you grab your shovel and start digging!

So a gongfermor had a disgusting, dangerous job that forced him to work nights and live outside the city walls. It sounds like a can't-get-any-worse situation. But there was one aspect of a gongfermor's job that wasn't poopy.

His wages.

Piggy Poop Disposals

Pigs need to eat. People need to poop. And in some areas of the world, these two facts of life came together in an unexpected way.

Instead of letting their poop hang out in a cesspit until a gongfermor lugged it away as was being done in medieval Europe, in areas of Asia a latrine was commonly built right over a pigsty. Poop in one of these bad boys and your feces would fall right into the pigs' feeding trough. You'd get rid of your poop and save money on pig food, all in one go!

Pig toilets like this were very common during the Han Dynasty in China (206 BCE–220 CE), but their use didn't die out when the last Han emperor was dethroned. In some areas of India, over 20 percent of the population were still using pig toilets in 2005.

LUCKY HUMANS... I WISH MY BUTT MADE FOOD.

121

Storming the Castle

If you set out to attack a castle during the Middle Ages, it wouldn't have been easy. Castles were typically built on high ground, meaning archers could rain arrows down upon you. The castle walls could be a whopping fifteen feet thick. And then there was the moat.

In movies and books, moats are frequently shown housing crocodiles or alligators, but this wasn't the case. They often contained something far worse: poop.

When the drawbridge was up, to reach the base of the castle, you'd have to swim through the sewage as arrows showered down upon your head. And if you somehow made it across, what next? You've just come face-to-face with the thick castle walls.

What was the castle's weakness? Look no further than the toilets themselves. Because you know those slanted garderobe poop chutes? They could be looked upon as unguarded entrances

to the castle! All you had to do was crawl up the stinky, slippery shaft and hope that no bare butts would be there to greet you when you reached the top.

Some armies—like that of King Philip II when he seized the Château Gaillard in France in 1204—*did* gain access to castles by using this unpleasant technique. As a result, many castles started fitting iron grates over their poop chutes to keep enemies outside where they belonged.

Every cesspit owner needed their cesspit emptied from time to time, and they sure didn't want to pull up their sleeves and do the dirty work themselves. Meaning those brave souls willing to do the job could charge a pretty penny. And I don't know about you, but I imagine they deserved every cent they got.

Q: Why did the gongfermor paint his poop wagon yellow?

A: So he could call it a stool bus!

You Did *What* with Your Poo?

Because dealing with cesspits is expensive and smelly, it's not surprising that the occasional person tried to find other ways to deal with their poo. People like Alice Wade, who illegally piped her waste not into her own cesspit but into a street gutter! This foul scheme of hers worked great . . . until her poop *clogged* the gutter and she was found out. Talk about awkward.

Even worse were the cheaters whose poop wasn't sent to the street or the gutter. But into their *neighbors'* cellars!

124

Chapter 11

From Pelt to Belt

Job: Tanner

Time Period: From Ancient Egypt Through the Nineteenth Century

A job called tanner doesn't sound all that bad. In fact, it sounds downright pleasant. Like you'd be getting paid to spend hour after hour frolicking outside in the sun's tanning rays.

But if the job of tanner was delightful, it wouldn't earn a chapter in this book. And tanners *most definitely* earned their place.

Their job was the pits.

By now you're probably wondering . . . if the word tanner didn't come from spending time in the sun, where did it come from? Well, it turns out that tanning has a lesser-known definition that deals with turning animal hides into leather. And this was the kind of tanning a tanner did.

Cows Are Only the Beginning

Most leather is made from cattle, but cows are definitely not alone. Horses, sheep, deer, hyenas. Pigs, buffalo, goats, yaks, bears. Alligators, crocodiles, snakes. Even stingray, kangaroo, and ostrich skins have been turned into leather!

As you might imagine, transforming animal skins into leather was a very important job. If people skipped this step—if they simply took the hide off a dead cow and sewed it into a coat—they'd have some real problems.

First of all, the coat would be hairy. Yuck! Second, there would still be all kinds of stuck-on fat and cow flesh. Double yuck! And third, because the skin wasn't processed, the coat would quickly start rotting away. In a matter of days, it would reek horrendously.

In other words, a coat like that would *not* earn you a seat at the cool table.

So how did a tanner turn a cow's hide into leather? Well, depending on whether he was working during the days of the pharaohs in Egypt, during the reign of Augustus in ancient Rome, during the days of the Black Death in the Middle Ages, or at the same time Alexander Graham Bell was inventing the telephone during the Victorian era, the exact details of the tanning process varied. But the first two steps were always the same: (1) Get your hands on an animal pelt, often with the help of the local butcher, and (2) wash the hide to get rid of any crusted-on blood, guts, poop, salt, or dirt.

Next, the tanner had to get the fur off the hide, because even during the days of Shakespeare nobody wanted a hairy belt. Unfortunately, though, it wasn't easy to remove the fur. The hairs wanted to stay where they were. The tanner needed to do something to loosen them up.

One method was to soak the pelt in a lime wash. But another frequently used technique was to leave the hides in a warm area until the flesh around the hair roots started to rot. To speed up the process, urine was often spread on the hides before leaving them out to decay.

Once a hide was deemed ready, the tanner would spread it over a wooden beam and use a blunt, double-handled knife to scrap away the hair. It was tough, backbreaking work. Often the pelt would need to take another swim in the lime wash or undergo another pee sprinkling or two before the tanner was able to achieve the desired freshly shaved appearance.

After the hair was gone, the tanner would flip the hide over and get to work on the other side. Knowing the market wasn't great for leather that still had globs of tissue attached to it, he took a sharp, two-handled knife and removed all the unwanted flesh.

Now that the hide was de-haired and de-fleshed, it was given a quick wash. Then it needed to go through a step to make sure the final leather would be nice and soft.

How did the tanner do this? With feces, of course. Often in the form of dog dung or pigeon droppings. The tanner would simply coat the hides with poop—or immerse them in a poo bath—and let everything simmer for a while. Before long, the enzymes in the poop would break down the proteins in the animal hides, making the leather softer, more flexible, and easier to work with.

To speed the process along, during the Victorian era steam pipes were sometimes laid under the dog poop pits to heat the mixture up. It was like an odoriferous, steamy dog-poop stew.

After the poop processing was done, the hides were washed again (thank goodness!). Then they'd take a quick bath in some tanning liquids before spending month after month in a large pit full of tanning materials like birch or oak bark.

But I Don't Want to Wear Cow!

Not everyone wants to build a snowman while wearing gloves made from the hide of a baby cow. Or line dance while sporting boots made from alligator skin. Or sit back and relax on a leather couch.

So there is an alternative for people who like the *appearance* of leather but not the animal death that goes along with it. That alternative is faux leather, or fake leather. You can buy furniture, purses, belts, suitcases, and all kinds of other products made out of cruelty-free leather substitutes.

Unfortunately, though, there's a catch. Faux leather is frequently made from non-biodegradable plastics that don't play nice with the environment, which means they're not always the best option either. But faux leather does have one diehard supporter: cows. Fake leather has them feeling over the moooo-n.

129

An entire year could pass before the leather would be deemed ready. It would then be pulled out of the pit, rinsed, smoothed, dried, and sold so it could be turned into something

Collecting Some Doggie Doo-Doo

GOOD DOG, THERE'S A GOOD DOG.

During the Victorian era, tanners used buttloads of dog dung when they made leather. But where did the poop come from? It sure would have been sweet if they'd had a crew of trained dogs that would poop in their poop pits like cats poop into litter boxes. But they didn't.

Luckily for them, though, there were lots of wild dogs roaming through the towns and villages. These dogs did their thing wherever and whenever they wanted, meaning there was tons of free poop lying around.

The tanners merely needed people willing to gather it up. People like pure collectors, whose job it was to go around collecting doggie doo-doo to sell to the tanners. Some pure collectors wore a glove on their poop-picking-up hand.

Others didn't bother.

Curious to know how pure collectors got their very paradoxical-sounding name? It turns out that dog feces was once commonly referred to as "pure"! Quite possibly because of the poop's role in purifying and softening leather.

marvelous. Like boots, saddles, pouches for carrying drinking water, or a 100 percent hair-free leather coat.

Pretty much everyone relied upon leather for one reason or another, but that didn't mean they wanted to get very close to a tanner or his workplace. And with all the rotting animal hides and urine and dung, it's no wonder why: the smell.

Most cities had strict restrictions regarding where a tanner could set up operations. Which makes sense. If a tanner moved next door to your family's bakery, your sales would plummet. Not even the prettiest-looking lemon tart could tempt a buyer if the air stunk like a bank of Porta Potties.

Come to think of it, all this talk about stinky rotten flesh and canine poo stew gives me a great business idea. Take a time machine. Travel back to the Victorian era. Visit a few tanners. And get rich.

Because they'd undoubtedly give you a fortune in exchange for a bottle of Febreze!

Q: After dealing with dog poop and rotting animal hides all day, how does the tanner keep from smelling when he goes home at night?

A: He plugs his nose!

The Blue Blues

Tanners were forced to do their work outside the city walls because of the stench. And they weren't alone. There were also rules about where a woad dyer could set up shop.

Woad is a flowering plant, and woad dyers had the job of processing the woad plant to make a dye that could turn wool from white to indigo—a bluish-violet color.

This might seem like an enjoyable enough job until you consider two things.

First, wool wasn't the only thing turning indigo. If you were a woad dyer, your hands, fingernails, and any other body parts exposed to the dye would also be stained blue. Which meant you'd spend most of your time walking around looking like Nebula from *Guardians of the Galaxy*.

And second, the woad-dying process apparently smelled like a cross between rotten cabbage and sewage. It smelled so putrid, in fact, that Queen Elizabeth I prohibited the processing of woad within *five miles* of anywhere she was staying. Five miles! That almost makes your sister's room-clearing farts seem innocent, doesn't it?

No Poop? How About Some Brains?

When tanners living in England during the Victorian era were simmering hides in warmed-up dog droppings, their goal was to soften the leather. Native Americans, on the other hand, had a different way to soften their hides: They used brains!

As the saying goes, "Every animal has just enough brains to tan its own hide." Which is mighty convenient for the person doing the tanning. And an unfortunate ill twist of fate for the poor animal.

133

Chapter 12

TP Holder for the King

Job: Groom of the Stool

Time Period: Sixteenth-Century England

King Henry VIII was much like a pair of dice—he had many sides.

There was Henry as a young boy. Born son number two, he was not supposed to end up on the throne. That job was meant for Arthur, his older brother. Arthur got the magnificent christening. Arthur got the more king-centric education. Arthur had his future wife picked out for him when he was two. But Henry went from spare to heir in the blink of an eye when Arthur died at age fifteen.

There was Henry as a young eighteen-year-old king. At slightly over six feet tall and strongly built, he was an imposing figure. An excellent hunter, dancer, and jouster, he was the perfect image of a kingly king. His court was festive. The people loved him.

There was Henry the husband. When wife number one failed to give him a son, he had their marriage annulled (declared invalid). This freed him up to marry again.

And again.

And again.

And again.

And again.

In total, Henry VIII married *six* times. He had two marriages annulled. Two wives beheaded. One wife died after childbirth. And then, surprise! His last wife managed to stay married to him—with her head still attached!—until his death.

And finally, there was Henry later in his reign. Cruel. Moody. In constant pain. He had to be carried around his palace in a chair because he could barely walk, and he sported oozing, seeping leg ulcers that could apparently be smelled from three rooms away.

Regardless of which of these versions of Henry VIII comes to your mind when you hear his name, once he was king he always employed a groom of the stool.

And no. The groom of the stool was not Henry's own personal mushroom taster, there to make sure the king wasn't served any poisonous toadstools.

And no. The groom of the stool did not follow the king around with a three-legged stool, ready at any moment to climb upon it if something needed to be fetched from a high, out-of-reach shelf.

Instead, the groom of the stool had the tremendous honor of accompanying the king anytime he needed to stool on his close stool.

Stool—as you may already know—is another name for poop. Like turds, feces, dung, excrement. And a close stool was essentially a toilet. It was shaped like a box with a large hole cut in the top. A person would sit on it and do their thing, and anything falling through the hole would plop into a perfectly situated chamber pot hidden inside the structure.

In King Henry's case, he had multiple different close stools at his various palaces. Not wanting to sit his butt on a hard surface, his close stools were cushioned using swan down feathers. They were also exquisitely decorated. One of his most famous toilets was covered in black velvet and bedecked with two thousand gilt nails and oodles of fringe.

Anytime the king needed to poo, he'd call upon his groom of the stool to go with him. The groom would hold the cloth

What to Do with the King's Poo

When King Henry VIII pooped or peed, his waste wasn't chucked into a moat or cesspit. At least not right away. Henry was terrified of illness, so he employed several personal physicians, royal apothecaries, and—at times—barber-surgeons. Every morning one of his physicians, dressed in their signature long, furry gown, would pay him a visit to make sure everything was okay. Part of the assessment? Analyzing the king's urine. And his poo!

that would serve as the king's toilet paper and make sure there was a basin, some water, and a towel all ready for afterward.

Depending on which account of the groom of the stool's job you read, some suggest the groom didn't merely hand the toilet paper to the king. He did the dirty work too! A royal butt wiper, if you will.

Accompanying the king anytime he had to empty his bowels seems like a terrible chore. The sounds. The smells. The

grunts. (And considering that King Henry VIII was often constipated, there must have been *a lot* of grunts!)

It's a job you'd think would land in the hands of the lowest
of servants. But you'd be wrong. It was a coveted position.

Why was this?

Because nobody else got to spend that much one-on-
one time with the king.

While the king was doing his business, he and his groom of
the stool could talk politics and wars. They could discuss the
upcoming jousting tournament and the queen's new dress.
The groom of the stool was in a great position to recommend
his friends for favorable positions within court. Or to hint that
so-and-so should not be trusted.

Not only that, the groom of the stool's position didn't end
when the king's butt left his close stool. The groom of the
stool got to help the king dress. He was in charge of the king's
jewels. He managed the finances of the king's household. He
supervised the king's private staff.

Basically, the groom of the stool made sure everything
within the king's personal living quarters was done properly.

And doing everything "properly" wasn't easy. It's been
reported that the simple act of getting King Henry's bed
ready each night required *ten* people.

Why ten? I have no clue. But there *were* a bunch of steps.

First, a dagger was plunged into the mattress to be sure
there were no king killers hiding in the straw. Then a layer of

The Great House of Easement

While King Henry VIII sat on his close stool at his Hampton Court Palace, where was everyone else doing their thing? VIPs could have their own quarters. And their own close stools. But if a person didn't rank that highly? They were supposed to use the Great House of Easement. This two-story public bathroom consisted of planks of wood with holes cut at cozy two-foot intervals. All the waste pooped through the openings went tumbling down angled chutes.

Everything was *supposed* to eventually empty into the River Thames, but given the hundreds of servants living at the palace whenever the king was in residence, over time the poo still built up. The Great House of Easement started smelling anything but great.

Because of the smell and because it was inconvenient to trek all the way to the Great House of Easement every time one had a full bladder, many servants apparently didn't bother. Much easier to just pee into a fireplace. Or behind a tree in the gardens. Or into a deserted hallway!

down was placed atop the mattress. Next, someone would roll up and down on the bed to make sure there were no sharp, dangerous objects concealed inside. Then the bed was made with fresh linens, blankets, and pillows.

After all the pillows were situated perfectly, everyone who'd participated in Operation Let's Make a Bed made the sign of the cross over the mattress. They kissed all the places they'd touched. And if we're early in King Henry VIII's reign, holy water was sprinkled upon the bed as well.

The king's sword and battle-ax were placed in the room in case an attacker entered the bedchamber that night. A close stool was set up for those times nature called at two in the morning. And then one of the men had to kneel by the bed, possibly for hours, guarding it until the king was ready to turn in for the night.

So yeah. The groom of the stool was an important job.

Off with His Head!

The Queen of Hearts—the villain from Lewis Carroll's *Alice's Adventures in Wonderland*—is probably the royal figure best known for ordering the beheading of her enemies. But King Henry VIII was no slouch. Not only did he behead two of his wives, but once it was his groom of the stool who found his head on the chopping block.

The groom of the stool in

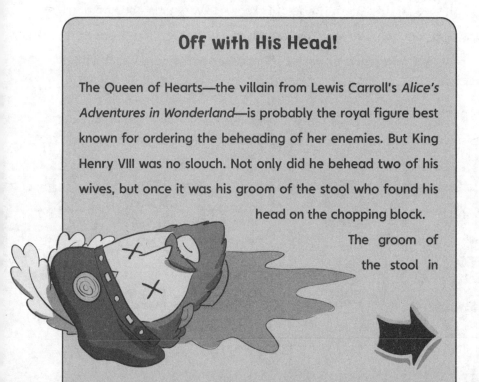

question was Henry Norris. He was once one of King Henry's closest confidants, but when the king decided he wanted to get rid of wife number two, Anne Boleyn, Norris's days were numbered. Anne was accused of having an affair with several men—including her musician, her own brother, and Norris—and it was "off with their head" for each and every one of them.

But I sure wouldn't want it. Because at the end of the day, he was still a TP holder. He had to smell the poo. He had to stand within inches of the king's reeking leg ulcers. It's very possible he had to *wipe* the royal backside.

And when the king was constipated—and was struggling and straining and grunting—the groom of the stool had to be the king's number one cheerleader. Or, if we want to be punny, his number two cheerleader!

Q: Why did Henry VIII's groom of the stool bring toilet paper to the party?

A: Because he knew the king was a party pooper!

Royal Enemas

When Henry VIII was all backed up and couldn't poop, sometimes he'd need a little help in the form of an enema. Don't know what an enema is? Consider yourself lucky. An enema typically involves sticking a tube up a person's backside and squirting a solution into their you-know-what. The goal is for the solution to make them poo. Enemas are still occasionally used to treat severe constipation today, but they used to be performed *way* more often. In Henry VIII's case, his groom of the stool once reported that the king had a "very fair siege" thanks to some laxatives and a particularly successful enema.

But Henry VIII's enema use was nothing compared to that of the Sun King, Louis XIV. King Louis—who took the throne in France in 1643 and ruled for a whopping seventy-two years—was *the* enema king. Rumor has it that he had more than two thousand enemas in his life, sometimes three or four in a single day.

And maybe there's something about King Louises in general because King Louis XIII reportedly had 212 enemas in a single year and King Louis XI made sure his pet *dogs* got enemas!

Chapter 13

A Poo Explosion

Job: Saltpeter Man

Time Period: Seventeenth Century and Thereabouts

When you stroll down a sidewalk, it's nice when people smile at you. Give you a quick wave. Or at least not glower at you as though you smell like a block of Limburger cheese.

But for the poor saltpeter men walking down the streets of Europe during the seventeenth century, this sure wasn't the case. Nobody wanted to see them. Sometimes they were even bribed to stay away.

This is because saltpeter men were sort of like FBI agents with a warrant in hand. If they knocked on your door, you had no choice but to let them inside. They could dig around in your house, your barn, your cellar. If they found anything interesting, they could take it. And if they left a mess? So be it.

Except the saltpeter men were not trying to uphold justice like the FBI agents. They weren't entering your house because you were suspected of doing something illegal. They weren't searching your home to see if you had a murder weapon hiding in your underwear drawer.

Nope. Saltpeter men came around to see if you had any saltpeter they could dig up and cart off.

Saltpeter. Odds are you have no clue what that is. It sure isn't a word that comes up often in normal twenty-first century conversation. But saltpeter, which can also go by its chemical name, potassium nitrate, used to be highly sought after.

Why was this? Because if you combined saltpeter with charcoal and sulfur, it made gunpowder—aka the stuff that made guns and cannons go *BOOM*.

Not surprisingly, kings and queens were desperate to get their hands on as much saltpeter as possible. They needed it so their olden-day army could kick other olden-day armies' butts.

Immortality? Or a Deadly Weapon?

Gunpowder is deadly. Swords and arrows were bad enough, but when gunpowder showed up on battlefields? Death and destruction was taken up about a gazillion notches.

Interestingly, though, gunpowder was not discovered by people looking for a powerful new weapon. It wasn't even found by people looking for a good way to kill.

It was discovered by people who wanted to *live*.

Forever.

Gunpowder is thought to have been invented by Chinese alchemists. Alchemy is when people try to transform one substance—like lead—into something else. Most often that "something else" was gold (which would make the alchemist rich) and an elixir of life (which would allow the alchemist to live f-o-r-e-v-e-r).

Lots of famous people from history were alchemists. Like Nicolas Flamel. And Isaac Newton.

While nobody ever succeeded in turning lead into gold, it's believed that Chinese alchemists discovered life-destroying gunpowder while looking for a path to immortality. Talk about doing a 180!

But where was a person to find this all-important saltpeter?

Unfortunately for saltpeter men, it couldn't be found growing from a tree. Or resting upon the sandy shores of a crystal-clear lake. Or in a field of wildflowers nestled between rugged, snowcapped mountains. Instead, saltpeter was found in locations where there was a lot of rotting organic matter. Especially rotting organic matter like animal poop. And animal pee.

Saltpeter Does More Than Go *Boom*

During the seventeenth century, saltpeter and gunpowder went hand in hand. Like peanut butter and jelly. Shoes and socks. Green eggs and ham.

Throughout history, though, saltpeter has actually been used in all kinds of different ways. It was used to preserve food. To desensitize sensitive teeth. To cure meat. It was used in agriculture. In glassmaking. As rocket fuel. And it was also a favorite ingredient among alchemists!

This meant that saltpeter men looked for their saltpeter in places like outhouses and pigeon coops and barns. If you're thinking this already sounds pretty bad, just wait. It gets worse. Because simply having poop and pee together wasn't enough. Potassium nitrate was only produced if the conditions were right.

If the area was exposed to lots of rain or sunlight? No saltpeter.

If there were plants around to consume the nitrates? No saltpeter.

If the chemicals and bacteria in the dirt and the poo weren't right? No saltpeter.

This meant that one outhouse could be a virtual saltpeter goldmine while the horse stable down the road had almost nothing. So how was a saltpeter man supposed to determine which ground was worth digging up and carting away? He did this by gaining entrance to a building. Digging up a bit of dirt. And testing it.

The "gaining entrance" part was easy. As we've already established, governments didn't want their armies running out of gunpowder. So they passed law after law that gave saltpeter men permission to dig anywhere they wanted. Even in their neighbor's outhouse. In the butcher's cellar. In the blacksmith's pigeon coop.

Then, once a saltpeter man was inside, he merely had to take a little sample and test it. But *how* did he test it? There were no soil labs around at that time to do fancy-schmancy chemical analyses for him, so the saltpeter man had to turn to something else. Like his very own well-tuned taste buds.

That's right.

The saltpeter man would *taste* the excrement-and-urine-rich dirt to see if it had the pungent, salty taste he was looking for.

If a particular sample wasn't promising, he'd move on to the next stable or cellar. The homeowner would let out a major sigh of relief.

Smelling the Moon

It's long been joked that the moon looks like a huge chunk of cheese. And in 1988, a survey performed by the Lowell Observatory in Flagstaff, Arizona, found that a whopping 13 percent of people actually believed the moon *was* made of cheese.

Given this long-standing moon–cheese association, it would be so fitting if the moon smelled like dairy products. But sadly, no. According to astronauts who've stood on the moon's surface, it smells like gunpowder.

So . . . is the moon the smelliest celestial body in our solar system? Not by a long shot. That award goes to those planets that are encased in clouds of hydrogen sulfide, a gas that smells like rotten eggs. And farts.

What is the greatest fart-smelling planet of them all? Uranus, of course!

HI, GUYS!

But if the earth looked (or rather tasted) good, he'd dig up a slew of it, lug it off in a wagon, and put the dirt through several processing steps to get out all the saltpeter. The kings and queens would be so pleased.

Or would they?

As it turns out, in many European countries the saltpeter obtained by digging up dovecotes and latrines and barnyards wasn't enough to keep up with demand. So to boost supply, saltpeter was frequently imported from other countries. Like India.

But even with these imports, there still often wasn't enough saltpeter around to keep armies in business. And when this happened, saltpeter was *made*.

How did a person go about making saltpeter? By copying the conditions where saltpeter was usually found, of course.

Peeing in the Pews

As saltpeter men went around digging up outhouses, pigeon coops, and stables, not surprisingly, people became angry. Complaints were made. Councils were summoned.

But one complaint stands out among the rest. In 1628, a case was made against Nicholas Stephens, a saltpeter man from England. Stephens didn't stop at digging up cellars and henhouses. Nope. He decided it was a good idea to dig up *churches*. In Chipping Norton, he and his men tore up a church so badly there were no places left for parishioners to sit or kneel.

When asked why, why, why digging up a church would ever be considered a good idea, Stephens's men insisted that churches were a great place for them to do their work. According to the workers, the women peed right in their seats, "which causes excellent saltpeter"!

Clay-lined trenches were filled with feces and urine and rotten vegetation. Every week a bunch of pee and liquidy poo and cesspit juices were added to keep everything nice and moist. Months or even years were allowed to pass so everything could "ripen." And then the material was processed to get out any saltpeter. As you can imagine, these saltpeter plantations were anything but smell-free. They were typically forced to be well outside town walls.

At the end of the day, it's clear . . . saltpeter men had a terrible job. They dealt with poop and pee all day long. They had to call upon their sense of taste in the most disgusting way. They were hated by all their neighbors. And worst of all? The material they produced was turned into gunpowder. Which killed countless people!

Q: Why wasn't the saltpeter man upset that he didn't have any friends in the neighborhood?
A: Because he still had his taste buds.

By Royal Decree: Save That Pee!

Before King Charles I was tried for treason and beheaded, he ruled England, Scotland, and Ireland from 1625 until 1649. During his time on the throne, he had quite a run. He angered his English subjects by marrying a Catholic. He dissolved Parliament over and over again so he could rule without its annoying interference, only to recall it again whenever he needed more cash. And he got England into war after war.

Because of these wars, King Charles I needed lots of gunpowder—and lots of saltpeter. To help with this, in 1626 the king issued the most interesting of declarations. He ordered his subjects to save their own pee, along with as much of their animals' urine as possible. The pee was then collected. And used to make saltpeter.

Chapter 14

The Ultimate Treasure Hunt!

Job: Tosher

Time Period: Nineteenth Century

"**P**rofessional treasure hunter" sounds like a dream job, doesn't it? Brings to mind Indiana Jones and his never-ending quest for priceless artifacts. Sure, Indy needs to deal with the occasional evil archeologist or heart-removing cult, but who cares? He gets adventure.

Travel to fascinating, far-off lands. And his very own bullwhip.

If searching for treasure sounds like your ideal occupation, too bad you didn't live in London, England, during the Victorian era—the time period from 1837 to 1901 when Queen Victoria sat upon the throne. You could have become a tosher, the ultimate treasure hunter of the day.

Then again, considering that toshers made it into this book, you know there has to be a catch. A downside. Some gross, disgusting twist.

And you'd be right.

Because a tosher's treasure wasn't nearly as exciting as a priceless artifact or long-lost relic. Toshers didn't get a bullwhip or signature hat. And instead of riding over waterfalls in amphibious vehicles or facing off against gigantic rolling boulders like Indiana Jones, a tosher dealt with toxic gas. And rats.

And the kicker? A tosher didn't search for treasure in exciting, far-off places. Their hunting grounds were much closer to home. In fact, their hunting grounds might be directly *below* their home.

Because a tosher searched for treasure . . . down in the sewers.

Sure doesn't sound like an ideal job anymore, does it?

It's hard to imagine why anyone would decide to trudge into a sewer, of all places, but in Victorian London, the gap between the haves and the have-nots was ginormous. On one hand, you had an upper class with elaborate balls, personal servants, and full stomachs. On the other hand, you had extreme poverty.

Mining the Sewers in the Twenty-First Century!

Chances are you don't consider your poop to be a treasure. But oddly enough, your poop might be worth something.

Nowadays we're surrounded by metal-containing products all the time, like makeup, detergents, pots and pans, hair products, and even the soil. The result of these exposures is that lots of minuscule bits of metal get flushed down toilets and drains and wind up in our sewers.

According to an article published in 2015 in the journal *Environmental Science & Technology*, if the metals in the biosolids of one million people were gathered together, they would be worth up to $13 million. A year!

Anyone interested in a field trip to the sewers?

I'll bring the metal detector.

URGH! WHAT? YEAH, STILL HERE, MA. OOF, IT'S LIKE I'M PASSING A STEEL GIRDER.

The slums were smelly and overcrowded. Beggars were everywhere. And poor, desperate mothers sometimes paid a "baby farmer" to take a child or two off their hands. The mother usually thought they were buying a better life for their kid, but after payment was collected, some baby farmers simply abandoned the children on the streets. Or killed them outright.

For much of London's population, life was a daily exercise of scraping by. Of doing whatever it took to survive another day.

In the case of a tosher, "doing whatever it took" meant heading down into the sewers. Early in the nineteenth century—when most poop was still collected in cesspits—the sewers weren't quite the places of poo they are today. It was actually against the law for Londoners to pipe their waste into them. But as the century wore on, this changed. Soon the stomping ground of the tosher was also the land of poop sludge, pee rivers, and sewer rats.

A day in the life of a tosher started with waiting for nightfall. It was illegal to enter the sewers without permission, so a tosher snuck in after dark.

Instead of a bullwhip, his "uniform" consisted of a coat that had multiple pockets to house any goodies he might find. He wore canvas pants and a canvas apron. He slung a bag over his shoulder, held a lantern to cut through the darkness, and carried a long pole with a hoe at the end.

The Lowdown on Victorian Underwear

If you were a wealthy lady living during the Victorian era, getting dressed would have been way more involved than pulling on some canvas trousers, a canvas apron, and a multi-pocketed coat like the toshers did. Fashions changed throughout the era, but getting ready likely included putting on a chemise, stockings, and some bloomers or pantaloons. You'd have a rib-squishing, stomach-pinching corset. You'd probably wear something to make your dress poof out, such as a hoop skirt; a wire structure called a cage crinoline; or one, two, three, even six petticoats.

And then, after all that, your dress would be pulled over your head and you'd yank on some fancy-looking but extremely uncomfortable boots. (Whatever you do, don't skip the boots! Otherwise there'd be nothing to protect your feet and ankles from all the horse poop, trash, and animal guts that often blanketed Victorian-era streets.)

With all that dressing, there was one thing you didn't put on: anything that resembles what we consider underwear today. There were no grannie panties. No boy shorts. No bikini briefs.

Everything was left open to the world, albeit safely hidden under layers upon layers of fabric.

Why wouldn't you wear any undies?

Because even back in the 1800s women needed to use a toilet from time to time. And lifting a virtual mountain of clothing while simultaneously trying to yank down a pair of underwear was a recipe for disaster. Sure, you might succeed once. Or twice. Or even three times. But eventually your luck would run out, you'd topple over, and boom. You'd wind up facedown in a chamber pot.

No. Thank. You.

By eliminating the whole underwear piece, all you had to do was lift your skirts. And go.

Hoo! Hooo! WHAT? NO, MOTHER, NO TROUBLE AT ALL.

It seems like a sewer treasure hunter would want to work on his own so any valuables he found would be his and his alone. But in actuality, toshers worked in groups of three or four. This was because entering the sewers alone was dangerous.

Death could come to a tosher in several ways:

- The sewer walls could crumble, trapping or crushing anyone in the area.

- A tosher might walk into a pocket of gas so toxic it could suffocate a rhino. And if the gas didn't asphyxiate him, it could cause an explosion.

- If he got lost or distracted and didn't get out before high tide, it could easily be lights out. The sewers often filled to the roof when the tide came in.

- And last but certainly not least, there was death by rats. The London sewers were swarming with rodents, and to them a lone tosher was like a wounded wildebeest to a pack of hungry lions. Sure, the tosher could swing and slash away with his pole, killing many, but eventually the sheer number of rats would overwhelm him. His body would be chewed away, bit by bit, until he was nothing more than a skeleton.

No wonder toshers adopted the buddy system!

As a group of toshers roamed around, they used their long poles to dig through all the filth that had washed into the sewers. Filth like human waste, rotten vegetables, and horse poop. There'd be putrid trash, dead animals, and foot after foot of pig guts that had been tossed out by slaughterhouses.

A Jaw-Dropping Victorian-Era Job

Digging through sewers and human excrement for bits of treasure sounds like a nightmarish job. By comparison, making matches in a factory sounds tame.

Matchsticks were exploding in popularity during the Victorian era, and why not? A tiny piece of wood that created a flame with the simple flick of the wrist? They must have seemed almost magical.

Unfortunately for the matchstick makers, however, things were not as bright for them. Most of the workers were poor women and children who worked for twelve or more hours a

day dipping little pieces of wood into a mixture containing white phosphorus. Their reward for doing such a tedious job was little pay; dark, cramped working conditions; and the possibility of developing phossy jaw.

Phossy jaw—which was caused by breathing in phosphorus fumes for hours on end—was the name given to a condition where a person's jaw and teeth started rotting away. It was painful. It was disfiguring. It smelled as bad as you would imagine dying, rotting flesh would smell. And it could happen after working only a few years as a matchstick maker.

In and among this foul refuse, the tosher looked for his treasure. Which might be a coin. A piece of jewelry. A bone. A marble. A spoon. It might be a scrap of rope or a piece of metal. Basically, his treasure was anything that could be scrubbed clean and sold for a profit.

What Stinks?

Do you have a nickname for your math teacher's vomit-inducing farts? You know the ones I'm talking about, right? The silent-but-deadly ones that Mr. Johnson lets out in the middle of class anytime he had broccoli salad for lunch. If not, I've got a nickname you can use (only in your head, of course! Don't *actually* say it out loud or you'll get detention!). That nickname is . . . the Great Stink.

Although, just so you know, Mr. Johnson's farts wouldn't be the first thing to be known by that name. There was also a Great Stink of 1858. That Great Stink occurred because early in the Victorian era, most of the poop pooped by the citizens of London eventually found its way into the River Thames.

Year after year, the Thames got browner. Stinkier. Fish that used to thrive in the waters died.

As you would expect, people complained. And legislators *did* occasionally debate what to do about the problem. But nothing much was done until 1858, one of the hottest summers on record. The sweltering heat that year magnified the stench billowing off the river, and the Houses of Parliament—which had recently been built upon the banks of the Thames—were treated to an unbearable odor.

The building's drapes were soaked in chloride of lime in an attempt to diminish the scent.

Lawmakers held handkerchiefs over their noses.

But still the air reeked.

With Parliament confronted so directly with the fumes, it's no surprise that they were finally moved to act. They appointed Joseph Bazalgette with the colossal task of constructing a new, bigger, more organized sewer system that could safely transport the poo out of town. The sewers took about ten years to build, but finally Londoners could breathe again.

Now if only there was such a solution to Mr. Johnson's Great Stink. Other than stealing his broccoli salad, that is.

In the end, clearly a tosher was not Indiana Jones. Indy didn't smell like poop. Indy feared snakes, not rats. And Indy didn't risk his life over a piece of poo-encrusted rope.

But there is no denying a tosher's job had a perk. In a

world where much of the population was struggling to make ends meet—where young children often got their first job before they turned seven—toshers made off relatively well. All the stuff they found and sold gave them enough cash to put them at the top of the working class.

So they weren't rich. They didn't have servants waiting on them hand and foot.

But they had more than most. And that was something.

 Q: What is a tosher's favorite breed of dog?
A: A golden retriever!

Being a Mudlark Was No Lark

Believe it or not, toshers were not the only treasure hunters in Victorian England. There were also the mudlarks. Mudlarks could be any age—from a bent-over old woman to a six-year-old boy—and they spent their days searching for anything sellable in the mud along the River Thames in London.

Unfortunately, as we've already learned in the section "What Stinks?" the Thames of the Victorian era didn't exactly have sparkling-clean waters. It was dreadfully polluted with sewage, which meant the mudlarks were scrounging around in a bunch of dirty poop water.

Mudlarks didn't have to face sewer rats or noxious gas like the toshers, but in all other ways their job was worse. The "treasures" they found, like lumps of coal, were worth well less than the treasures found by toshers. This meant their bellies were frequently empty and they couldn't afford to wear anything but rags.

They often waded knee-deep through the muddy water with no shoes on their feet. If they stepped on a sliver of glass or a piece of sharp metal, they could easily wind up with a nasty cut. And given the lack of antibiotics and their poop-filled hunting grounds, even the simplest cut could turn into a raging infection.

Which could spell death.

Chapter 15

The Bird Poop Blues

Job: Guano Collector

Time Period: Nineteenth Century

Off the coast of Peru lie three tiny islands called the Chincha Islands. The temperature there hovers around seventy degrees all year round. Countless seabirds nest upon the shores. And rain falls so rarely that an entire lifetime can pass between downpours. On the surface these islands sound like the perfect place to go for spring break, but maybe wait a second before buying your plane ticket.

Why wait? Because all those seabirds living there do the same thing every other animal does: They excrete their waste. And over hundreds and thousands of years, that seabird poop—called guano—could really pile up. By the beginning of the nineteenth century, there were areas on the islands where the guano was two hundred feet deep! That's taller than Cinderella's castle in Disney World!

Wow! That's a Lot of Poo!

The Chincha Islands are tiny. The largest of the three is less than a mile long. But the bird poop was once piled so thick that in 1857 alone more than 980 *million* pounds of guano was mined from the islands. That's how much 327,000 female hippos weigh!

And between 1851 and 1872? More than twenty *billion* pounds of guano left the islands. That's more than six and a half *million* hippos.

Talk about a *lot* of poo!

As it turns out, those guano mountains were great news for the people who owned the islands at the time. This is because guano is chock-full of nitrogen and phosphorus, the nutrients found in fertilizer. Farmers were willing to pay major bucks for the stuff. Guano was so sought after, in fact, that wars were fought over it.

Now to be fair, the Chinchas were not alone in having guano. Bird poo could be found on islands all around the world. But the guano on the Chincha Islands was special. It put all that other guano to shame. Big time. This was for a couple reasons.

First of all, the ocean currents running past the Peruvian islands were bursting with fish. These fish supported a massive seabird population that was free to poop, poop, poop away. And second, the lack of rain on the Chincha Islands meant the guano could bake in the sun—completely undisturbed—for decade after decade. Everywhere else periodic rainfalls washed away much of the nitrates, thus making the guano less useful.

Simply put, in the days before cheap, man-made chemical fertilizers, guano from the Chincha Islands was the crème de la crème. The bee's knees. The cat's pajamas.

There was one major problem, though: how to get the priceless guano off the islands. As you might imagine, it wasn't as simple as grabbing a shovel and digging away. The guano on the islands had been building up for millennia. It was firmly packed down and had essentially turned into poop rocks.

This meant the guano collectors needed to *mine* it.

Explosive Bat Dung

In this chapter, it's guano from seabirds that's getting all the attention, but bat poo is called guano as well. And it also played an important role in history.

In chapter 13, we learned all about the saltpeter men who'd search outhouses and stables for saltpeter that could be turned into gunpowder. Well, in the United States, these weren't the only places saltpeter was found. It was also found in bat-infested limestone caves.

During the American Civil War, the Confederacy's gunpowder supplies relied heavily on guano-rich caves for their saltpeter!

At various times during the guano boom, the poop might have been dug up using pickaxes or crowbars or dynamite. Deep trenches, which could be more than one hundred feet deep, were dug to get better access to the good-as-gold poo.

It was backbreaking, smelly work performed under the brutal rays of the sun. But that's not the worst of it. It was also dangerous.

Ammonia fumes caused blindness. Trenches caved in. Nosebleeds, respiratory distress, abdominal pains, nausea, and diarrhea were common among the workers.

If you consider that guano collectors had to risk their lives to dig up a bunch of bird poo, who would want the job?

Answer: nobody.

Well, okay. So a few people signed on for pay. But they were the exception. Almost all the workers were there against their will. Convicts. Enslaved people. Army deserters. And Chinese workers who'd been tricked into coming.

These Chinese laborers had agreed to jump on a ship, leave China, and work for a set number of years in exchange for something. Most often that promised "something" was fair wages followed by a return trip home. In reality, though, once the ships left China's shores, there was no going back. The workers had been lied to.

Between 1849 and 1875, more than ninety thousand Chinese laborers arrived in Peru. Thousands more died on the ships taking them there. Most of the workers ended up serving on plantations. Some built railroads. But the most unlucky of the bunch found themselves on the Chincha Islands.

Once there, they faced more than compacted poop piles and poisonous fumes. They were forced to work long hours, day after day, with way too little food in their bellies. They had nothing but grass mats as beds. They had cruel work masters who'd punish them if they didn't mine enough guano in any given day. Punishment could mean being whipped. Being tied to a buoy. Or having a half-starved dog set loose on them.

Making Do with What You've Got

If you've been wondering what varieties of seabird species poop a poop so wonderful that people fought wars over it, the answer is the Peruvian pelican, the Peruvian booby, and, most important, the Guanay cormorant.

Guanay cormorants are black-and-white birds that stand about two-and-a-half-feet tall. While they love the Chincha Islands because of the endless seafood buffet just offshore, when it comes time to build their nests, the selection of building materials is sparse. There are no trees. No shrubs. No bushes. And any rocks, pebbles, or sand grains have long ago been covered with layer upon layer of bird excrement.

So what do the cormorants do? They use something they do have easy access to: poop. Nothing says home sweet home, after all, quite like your very own poop nest.

Perhaps cruelest of all was that this brutal, endless work was done within sight of the beautiful country of Peru, with its rugged coastline and lush green mountains. Ships passed by frequently, the passengers free. Like the Chinese workers used to be. And like they still should have been.

With all hope of a happy future gone, it's not surprising that many Chinese men died by suicide. Countless others were killed by the job itself.

The plight of these Chinese guano collectors is unbearably sad. Every one of those men had hopes, dreams, and goals, but their lives were stolen from them for the sake of money and power. Who knows? One of those men might have become the next Isaac Newton. Or made a medical discovery that would have saved countless lives. But we'll never know, will we, because their lives were deemed unimportant simply because of where they were born.

And unfortunately, discrimination is still going on all around us today. Discrimination based on the color of a person's skin. Or their country of origin. Discrimination based on gender or sexuality. Discrimination based on which god a person prays to at night.

None of this is okay.

We are *all* humans. We live on the same planet. We orbit the same sun. We all eat. We all sleep. We all fart.

We are so much more alike than we are different.

And if more of us could remember this? Man, what a beautiful world this could be.

Q: What did the bird say to the man collecting his guano?

A: You can take my poop, but I'm sure not taking yours!

Famous Poop Islands

Back during the guano boom days, everyone seemed to want in on the bird poop action. Even the United States. In 1856, the United States passed the Guano Islands Act, which allowed it to lay claim to any guano-covered island or rock it wanted, provided it wasn't already owned by another country.

Most people assumed that the claims to these islands were temporary. That once the guano had been mined, the islands would be released back to the wild. But not all the islands were given up. And some have gone on to play an important role in US history.

Like Midway Atoll. This island was the location of the Battle of Midway, the major air–sea battle between the United States and Japan during World War II. This battle is often looked upon as one of the war's major turning points.

Then there is Howland Island. This is the tiny island in the Pacific Ocean where Amelia Earhart was planning to refuel in 1937 during her attempt to fly around the world. She disappeared while looking for it.

And let's not forget about Johnston Atoll, which has quite the military history. It's been a naval air base, a staging area for nuclear tests, a storage area for Agent Orange and mustard gas, and a test site for biological weapons. In other words, it would not make a very good honeymoon destination.

Chapter 16

Born Unlucky

Job: Manual Scavenger
Time Period: Now

In chapter 10, we learned about gongfermors. How they went around cleaning poop out of backyard cesspits and castle moats during the Middle Ages. There's no way around it: It was disgusting work.

But what if I told you that now, in the twenty-first century, people are *still* doing almost the exact same job?

And no, I'm not talking about the sewer workers who keep the poop tunnels under New York City and San Francisco working. Those people are undeniably heroic for facing feces and sewer gas in their quest to make sure our poo gets where it needs to go, but—unlike the gongfermors—sewer workers in the United States get protective equipment.

Like goggles, liquid-repelling overalls, and waterproof gloves. Rubber boots and protective face shields. Sometimes hazmat suits, safety harnesses, and breathing devices. The goal of all this equipment is to keep the workers safe.

But there are poop handlers in India who don't get any of this protection. They're called manual scavengers, and their job is to clean up other people's excrement.

For men, the job often entails climbing into sewers and septic tanks to empty out the waste. They routinely wind up waist-deep, chest-deep, even neck-deep in feces.

For women, the job usually involves going from house to house to pick up—often with their bare hands—all the poop that's accumulated there since the previous day. They deposit the feces in a basket or bucket, which they lug around from place to place until it's full. Then the contents are cast into designated dumping grounds.

A lot of manual scavengers have also found work with the railways over the years. This is because the passenger trains that crisscross India every day once all had toilets that let poop simply plop right onto the ground. Manual scavengers then walked along the tracks and cleaned up the waste.

The job of manual scavenger sounds so horrific, it's hard not to wonder how a person could ever wind up in that line of work in the first place. Well, it's largely thanks to India's more than two-thousand-year-old caste system.

A caste system basically divides a population into groups. In India, a child would be born into the caste of their parents, and that's where they would stay.

Forever.

Historically it didn't matter one bit how smart they were. It didn't matter how motivated they were. It didn't matter what they enjoyed doing in their spare time—if they had any spare time.

People lived among members of their same caste. Married a person from their own caste. Did a job deemed acceptable for their caste.

In a super-simplified look at the Indian caste system, the Brahmins were at the tippy-top. They were the priests and scholars. Next came the Kshatriyas, the rulers and warriors. Following them were the Vaishyas, the merchants and land-owners. And then there were the Shundras, who were the peasants and servants.

But wait. There was one more group. A group so lowly that many didn't even consider it part of the caste system.

This group is now officially called the Scheduled Caste, but over time it has been referred to by many other names. Like Dalit. Harijan. And the cruelest name imaginable: the Untouchables.

As offensive as the name "Untouchable" is, it's sadly a descriptive one. Members of the Scheduled Caste were kept separate from everyone else. They frequently were not allowed into stores. Most villages didn't want them living nearby. Doctors commonly turned their backs on them.

If they touched food, the food was considered unclean. If they touched water, the water became unclean.

As you might imagine, not many jobs were open to an "untouchable" person. But manual scavenging was one they could do.

Nowadays there is supposed to be no such thing as a manual scavenger. The job has been declared *illegal*. But just because it's illegal doesn't mean people don't do it. For many families trapped by poverty and discrimination, it's their only option.

The Department of Social Justice and Empowerment's 2020–2021 annual report identified 66,692 manual scavengers across India, but the *actual* number of people doing this demeaning work is assumed to be much, much higher.

And sadly, the job isn't only repugnant. It's also super dangerous. Thanks to the noxious fumes, lack of protective equipment, and exposure to countless bacteria and other germs,

Potty Privilege

If you're like me, you have a toilet—or maybe two or three toilets—right in your own home. This might sound pathetic when compared to Buckingham Palace's *seventy-eight* bathrooms, but even so we're extremely lucky.

Around the world 3.6 *billion* people (as in almost half of the world's population!) do not have a single safe, well-functioning toilet in their abode. And some of these people have no choice but to poop in the bushes. By train tracks. Into plastic bags.

Not surprisingly, in places where people have to go without toilets, poop—and all the worms, bacteria, and viruses found within that human waste—can end up everywhere. Including in the drinking water. In fact, it's estimated that a whopping two billion people worldwide use drinking water that is contaminated with feces.

What's the end result of drinking that contaminated water? Lots and lots of poop-related deaths.

In March 2022, the World Health Organization estimated that inadequate sanitation causes 485,000 deaths due to diarrhea. Every year! That's almost one death every minute. Sadly, most of the victims are infants and young children.

So the next time someone asks what you're most thankful for, after giving thanks for your darling sister whom you love above all else, consider giving a quick shout-out to good old-fashioned sanitation.

Swimming Through Poo

If you love scuba diving because it's exciting—and not because you enjoy seeing the colorful little fishies—have I got a job for you.

Sewer diver!

Sewer divers are called upon when there is a blockage or structural problem in a sewer that's so deep it literally requires a person to swim through the poop pipes to reach it.

Unlike the manual scavengers in India, though, sewer divers get protection. They put on a suit that covers every square inch of their body to protect them from the poop, pee, toilet paper, garbage, and floating dead rat corpses they'll be swimming through. They get attached to a hose that sends them fresh air and allows them to communicate with a support crew waiting on the surface.

In many ways, they are like the men on *Stranger Things* who get all garbed up in orange hazmat suits before heading into the

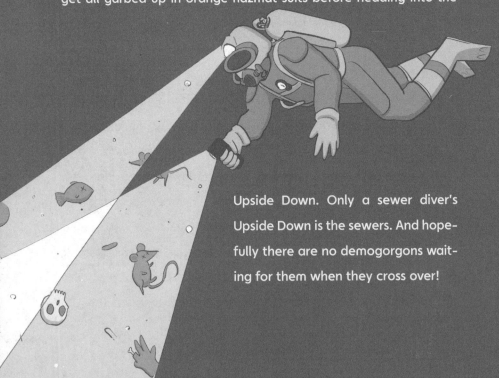

Upside Down. Only a sewer diver's Upside Down is the sewers. And hopefully there are no demogorgons waiting for them when they cross over!

manual scavenging just might be the most hazardous job on the planet today. Between 2015 and 2020, India's government reported that 340 people died while cleaning sewers and septic tanks. This translates to one person dying every five or six *days*. And while this figure is mind-blowing enough, it's almost certainly an underestimation. In 2023, the Safai Karmachari Andolan—a human rights organization fighting for the complete elimination of manual scavenging—estimated on its website that more than six hundred manual scavengers die every year!

The fact that manual scavenging still happens in the twenty-first century, that a job exists where a person has to handle human feces without gloves or goggles or other protections, is beyond upsetting. It's wrong on so many levels.

But there is some hope. There are areas of India—especially the larger cities—where a good education and quality jobs are no longer strictly limited to the upper classes. There are now politicians, lawyers, and doctors from the Scheduled Caste.

Not only this, but as more people learn about manual scavengers and their horrendous working conditions, change is coming. For example, in 2021 Indian Railways announced that it had finished installing bio-toilets in all its long-distance trains. These bio-toilets are not without problems, but they do at least succeed in cutting down on the amount of feces littered across the train tracks for manual scavengers to clean up.

This means that things finally seem to be moving on the right track, even if the pace of that change is painfully slow.

Q: There are two reasons why a sewer diver should never drink the sewage. What are they?

A: Number one. And number two.

US SEWERS CIRCLE THE DRAIN

Almost Flunking Out

Every four years, the American Society of Civil Engineers grades the US infra-structure. And in 2021, our wastewater system did not earn an A.

Or a B.

Or a C.

Or even a C-.

It got a D+!

Which puts it solidly in no-cell-phone-or-video-games-for-a-month territory!

Then again, at least our wastewater system scored better than our transit system. It barely squeaked by with a D-.

REPORT CARD

WATER: DRINKING	C-
WATER: WASTE	D+
WATER: STORM	D
LEVEES	D
DAMS	D
BRIDGES	C

See me after class!

Rain, Rain, Go Away!

A good, hard rain can seem cleansing. The dirt and grime on our sidewalks and cars get washed away. The grass turns brighter. Greener.

But I'm going to let you in on a dirty little secret. In approximately 700 communities across the United States—most of them in the bigger, older cities—wastewater and rainwater get channeled into the same water treatment system. These combined systems are cheaper to build, and when there isn't much rain, they work great. All the waste-water in the sewers flows properly into a treatment center.

But what happens if there's a heavy rain?

The system gets overwhelmed. It can't handle both the poopy sewer water *and* the rainwater, so much of the waste bypasses the water treatment center entirely. The outcome: A whole lot of toilet water pours straight into local waterways. Without under-going *any* treatment first!

The Homestretch

Phew! We have now officially survived our exploration of some of the grossest jobs throughout history. We've watched gongfermors jump into cesspits, experienced a scream-filled day in the life of a barber-surgeon, and waded out into a bog with a leech collector. It wasn't always pleasant, but hopefully you've had as much fun *learning* about these jobs as I had *writing* about them!

Although . . . reading about all these occupations has probably got you thinking about your own future. What job—or jobs—will you end up doing? If you find maggots fascinating, maybe you'll become a forensic entomologist! Or if you relish the thought of looking up noses all day long, perhaps a career as an allergist is for you. Or if you prefer to sit in your own house surrounded by overflowing bookcases, maybe you'll become an author. But whatever you do, I truly hope you find a job that Brings You Joy. My best advice? Dream big, study hard, find what *YOU* love (even if others find it disgusting), and reach for the stars!

Selected Bibliography

Chapter 1: Mummy Making

"Animal Mummies." *NOVA*. Season 42, Episode 11. PBS. October 28, 2015.

Antelme, Ruth Schumann, and Stéphane Rossini. *Becoming Osiris: The Ancient Egyptian Death Experience*. Translated by Jon Graham. Rochester, NY: Inner Traditions International, 1998.

Black, Winston. "Animated Corpses and Bodies with Power in the Scholastic Age." In *Death in Medieval Europe: Death Scripted and Death Choreographed*, edited by Joëlle Rollo-Koster. London: Taylor & Francis, 2017.

Brier, Bob. *Egyptian Mummies: Unraveling the Secrets of an Ancient Art*. New York: William Morro and Company, 1994.

Brier, Bob. *The History of Ancient Egypt*. The Great Courses lecture series.

Brier, Bob, and Hoyt Hobbs. *Ancient Egypt: Everyday Life in the Land of the Nile*. New York: Sterling, 2009.

Budge, E. A. Wallis. *The Egyptian Book for the Dead*. London: Penguin Classics, 2008 edition.

David, Rosalie, and Rich Archbold. *Conversations with Mummies: New Light on the Lives of Ancient Egyptians*. Toronto: Madison Press, 2000.

Fletcher, Joanne. *The Story of Egypt: The Civilization That Shaped the World*. New York: Pegasus Books, 2016.

Haywood, John, ed. *Life in the Ancient World: A History of How People Lived*. London: Lorenz Books, 2008.

Ikram, Salima, and Aidan Dodson. *The Mummy in Ancient Egypt: Equipping the Dead for Eternity*. London: Thames and Hudson, 1998.

Roach, Mary. *Stiff: The Curious Lives of Human Cadavers*. New York: W. W. Norton & Company, 2003.

Quigley, Christine. *The Corpse: A History*. Jefferson, NC: McFarland & Company, 1996.

Williams, A. R. "Animals Everlasting: Wrapped in Linen and Reverently Laid to Rest, Animal Mummies Hold Intriguing Clues to Life and Death in Ancient Egypt." *National Geographic*, November 2009.

Chapter 2: For the Love of Leeches

Becker, Norbert, Dušan Petrić, Marija Zgomba, Clive Boase, Christine Dahl, Minoo Madon, and Achim Kaiser. *Mosquitos and Their Control*, 2nd ed. Heidelberg: Springer, 2010.

Belofsky, Nathan. *Strange Medicine: A Shocking History of Real Medical Practices Through the Ages*. New York: Penguin Group, 2013.

Dawson, Ian. 2005. *Medicine in the Middle Ages*. New York: Enchanted Lion Books, 2005.

"Galápagos tortoises." *National Geographic*. https://www.nationalgeographic.com/animals/reptiles/g/galapagos-tortoise/.

George, Rose. *Nine Pints: A Journey Through the Money, Medicine, and Mysteries of Blood*. New York: Metropolitan Books, 2018.

Kutschera, U., and P. Wirtz. "The Evolution of Parental Care in Freshwater Leeches." *Theory Bioscience* 120 (2001): 115–37.

Millingen, J. G. *Curiosities of Medical Experience*. London: Richard Bentley, 1839.

Newquist, H. P. *The Book of Blood: From Legends and Leeches to Vampires and Veins*. New York: Houghton Mifflin Books for Children, 2012.

Palmer, Jane. "The Creatures that Can Survive Without Water for Years." *BBC*. September 27, 2016. https://www.tjanepalmer.com/wp-content/uploads/2021/10/BBC-Earth-The-creatures-that-can-survive-without-water-for-years.pdf

Pickover, Clifford A. *The Medical Book: From Witch Doctors to Robot Surgeons, 250 Milestones in the History of Medicine*. New York: Sterling, 2012.

Robinson, Tony. *The Worst Jobs in History: Two Thousand Years of Miserable Employment*. London: Pan Books, 2004

Stromberg, Joseph. "How Does the Tiny Waterbear Survive in Outer Space?" *Smithsonian Magazine*. September 11, 2012. https://www.smithsonianmag.com/science-nature/how-does-the-tiny-waterbear-survive-in-outer-space-30891298/.

Chapter 3: A Jack of All Trades

Albee, Sarah. *Poop Happened! A History of the World from the Bottom Up.* New York: Walker & Company, 2010.

Anderson, Julie, Emm Barnes, and Emma Shackleton. *The Art of Medicine: Over 2,000 Years of Images and Imagination.* Chicago: The University of Chicago Press, 2011.

Belofsky, Nathan. *Strange Medicine: A Shocking History of Real Medical Practices Through the Ages.* New York: The Penguin Group, 2013.

Dobson, Mary. *The Story of Medicine: From Bloodletting to Biotechnology.* London: Quercus, 2013.

Fabbri, Christiane Nockels. "Treating Medieval Plague: The Wonderful Virtues of Theriac." *Early Science and Medicine* 12, no. 3 (2007): 247–83. http://www.jstor.org/stable/20617676.

George, Rose. *Nine Pints: A Journey Through the Money, Medicine, and Mysteries of Blood.* New York: Metropolitan Books, 2018.

González-Crussí, F. *A Short History of Medicine.* New York: Modern Library, 2007.

Goodrich, Jean N. "Fairy, Elves and the Enchanted Otherworld." *Handbook of Medieval Culture Volume 1*, edited by Albrecht Classen. Berlin: De Gruyter, 2015.

History.com editors. *History of Witches.* September 19, 2019. https://www.history.com/.amp/topics/folklore/history-of-witches.

Hollingham, Richard. *Blood and Guts: A History of Surgery.* New York: Thomas Dunne Books, 2008.

Kelly, Kate. *The History of Medicine: The Middle Ages (500–1450).* New York: Facts On File, 2009.

Kelly, Kate. *The History of Medicine: The Scientific Revolution and Medicine (1450-1700).* New York: Facts On File, 2010.

Millingen, J. G. *Curiosities of Medical Experience.* London: Richard Bentley, 1839.

Mortimer, Ian. *The Time Traveler's Guide to Medieval England—A Handbook for Visitors to the Fourteenth Century*. New York: Touchstone, 2008.

Parker, Steve. *Kill or Cure: An Illustrated History of Medicine*. New York: DK Publishing, 2013.

Pickover, Clifford A. *The Medical Book: From Witch Doctors to Robot Surgeons, 250 Milestones in the History of Medicine*. New York: Sterling, 2012.

Porter, Roy. *Blood & Guts: A Short History of Medicine*. New York: W. W. Norton & Company, 2003.

Robinson, Tony. *The Worst Jobs in History: Two Thousand Years of Miserable Employment*. London: Pan Books, 2004.

Wynbrandt, James. *The Excruciating History of Dentistry*. New York: St. Martin's Press, 1998.

Chapter 4: The Dead Rise

Anderson, Julie, Emm Barnes, and Emma Shackleton. *The Art of Medicine: Over 2,000 Years of Images and Imagination*. Chicago: The University of Chicago Press, 2011.

Bailey, James Blake. *The Diary of a Resurrectionist: 1811–1812, to Which Are Added an Account of the Resurrection Men in London and a Short History of the Passing of the Anatomy Act*. London: Swan Sonnenschein & Co., 1896.

Belofsky, Nathan. *Strange Medicine: A Shocking History of Real Medical Practices Through the Ages*. New York: Penguin Group, 2013.

Bondeson, Jan. *Buried Alive: The Terrifying History of Our Most Primal Fear*. New York: W. W. Norton & Company, 2001.

González-Crussí, Frank. *A Short History of Medicine*. New York: Modern Library, 2007.

Parker, Steve. *Medicine: The Definitive Illustrated History*. New York: DK Publishing, 2016.

Pickover, Clifford A. *The Medical Book: From Witch Doctors to Robot Surgeons, 250 Milestones in the History of Medicine*. New York: Sterling, 2012.

Porter, Roy. *Blood & Guts: A Short History of Medicine*. New York: W. W. Norton & Company, 2003.

Selected Bibliography

Quigley, Christine. *The Corpse: A History*. Jefferson, NC: McFarland & Company, 1996.

Roach, Mary. *Stiff: The Curious Lives of Human Cadavers*. New York: W. W. Norton & Company, 2003.

Robinson, Tony. *The Worst Jobs in History: Two Thousand Years of Miserable Employment*. London: Pan Books, 2004.

Chapter 5: Watching the Dead Rot

Andrews, Travis M. "Chopin Wanted His Heart Cut Out and Preserved. Now It May Have Resolved the Mystery of His Death." *The Washington Post*, November 10, 2017.

Belofsky, Nathan. *Strange Medicine: A Shocking History of Real Medical Practices Through the Ages*. New York: Penguin Group, 2013.

Bondeson, Jan. *A Cabinet of Medical Curiosities*. Ithaca, NY: Cornell University Press, 1997.

Bondeson, Jan. *Buried Alive: The Terrifying History of Our Most Primal Fear*. New York: W. W. Norton & Company, 2001.

Colman, Penny. *Corpses, Coffins, and Crypts: A History of Burial*. New York: Henry Holt & Company, 1997.

Crippen, David W., ed. *End-of-Life Communication in the ICU: A Global Perspective*. New York: Springer, 2008.

"Full Text of Alfred Nobel's Will." *The Nobel Media*. 2022. https://www.nobelprize.org/alfred-nobel/full-text-of-alfred-nobels-will-2/.

Gould, Francesca. *Why Fish Fart & Other Useless or Gross Information About the World*. New York: Jeremy P. Tarcher/Penguin, 2009.

Roach, Mary. *Stiff: The Curious Lives of Human Cadavers*. New York. W. W. Norton & Company: 2003.

Tebb, William, Edward Perry Vollum, and Walter R. Hedwen. *Premature Burial: How It May Be Prevented*. Edited by Jonathan Sale. London: Hesperus Press Limited, 1905.

Quigley, Christine. *The Corpse: A History*. Jefferson, NC: McFarland & Company, 1996.

Wullschlager, Jackie. *Hans Christian Andersen: The Life of a Storyteller*. New York: Alfred A. Knopf, 2000.

Chapter 6: When Maggots Tell Time

Bass, Bill, and Jon Jefferson. *Beyond the Body Farm: A Legendary Bone Detective Explores Murders, Mysteries, and the Revolution in Forensic Science.* New York: HarperCollins, 2007.

Bass, Bill, and Jon Jefferson. *Death's Acre: Inside the Legendary Forensic Lab the Body Farm Where the Dead Do Tell Tales.* New York: G. P. Putnam's Sons, 2003.

Craig, Emily. *Teasing Secrets from the Dead: My Investigations at America's Most Infamous Crime Scenes.* New York: Crown Publishers, 2004.

Erzinclioglu, Zakaria. *Maggots, Murder, and Men: Memories and Reflections of a Forensic Entomologist.* New York: Thomas Dunne Books, 2000.

Forensic Anthropology Center, University of Tennessee. Accessed November 29, 2022. http://fac.utk.edu/collections-and-research/.

Goff, M. Lee. *A Fly for the Prosecution: How Insect Evidence Helps Solve Crimes.* Cambridge, MA: Harvard University Press, 2000.

Gould, Francesca. *Why Fish Fart & Other Useless or Gross Information About the World.* New York: Jeremy P. Tarcher/Penguin, 2009.

Greenberg, Bernard, and John C. Kunich. *Entomology and the Law: Flies as Forensic Indicators.* Cambridge, UK: Cambridge University Press, 2002.

McDermid, Val. *Forensics: What Bugs, Burns, Prints, DNA, and More Tell Us About Crime.* New York: Grove Press, 2014.

Platt, Richard. *Crime Scene: The Ultimate Guide to Forensic Science.* New York: DK Publishing, 2003.

Sachs, Jessica Snyder. *Corpse: Nature, Forensics, and the Struggle to Pinpoint Time of Death.* Cambridge, MA: Perseus Publishing, 2001.

Chapter 7: Bedpan, Anyone?

American Red Cross. "Red Cross Nursing: Strengthening Community Resiliency." 2022. https://www.redcross.org/about-us/who-we-are/history/nursing.html.

Belofsky, Nathan. *Strange Medicine: A Shocking History of Real Medical Practices Through the Ages.* New York: Penguin Group, 2013.

Selected Bibliography

Brier, Bob, and A. Hoyt Hobbs. *Daily Life of the Ancient Egyptians.* Westport, CT: Greenwood Press, 2008.

González-Crussí, Frank. *A Short History of Medicine.* New York: Modern Library, 2007.

Multiple personal interviews with nursing assistants, including Shannon Lauengco and Melissa Labrosse.

Pliny the Elder. *Natural History.* Translated by Perseus Digital Library. Accessed December 2022. https://www.perseus.tufts.edu/hopper/text?doc=Perseus%3Atext%3A1999.02.0137%3Abook%3D30%3Achapter%3D9.

Chapter 8: It's a Puke Party!

Carter, W. Hodding. *Flushed: How the Plumber Saved Civilization.* New York: Atria Books, 2006.

Cowell, F. R. *Everyday Life in Ancient Rome.* London: B.T. Batsford, 1961.

Dunbabin, Katherine. *The Roman Banquet: Images of Conviviality.* Cambridge, UK: Cambridge University Press, 2003.

Forsyth, Mark. *Horologicon: A Day's Jaunt Through the Lost Words of the English Language.* New York: The Berkley Publishing Group, 2013.

Harvey, Brian K. *Daily Life in Ancient Rome: A Sourcebook.* Indianapolis, IN: Hackett Publishing Company, 2016.

Hill, Duncan. *Ancient Rome: From the Republic to the Empire.* Bath, UK: Parragon Books, 2010.

Laurence, Ray. *Roman Passions: A History of Pleasure in Imperial Rome.* London: Continuum, 2009.

Nardo, Don. *Arts, Leisure, and Entertainment: Life of the Ancient Romans.* Farmington Hills, MI: Lucent Books, 2004.

Robinson, Tony. *The Worst Jobs in History: Two Thousand Years of Miserable Employment.* London: Pan Books, 2004.

Shelton, Jo-Ann. *As the Romans Did: A Sourcebook in Roman Social History,* 2nd ed. New York: Oxford University Press, 1998.

Chapter 9: My, What a Beautiful Toga You Have!

Ekarius, Carol, and Deborah Robson. *The Fleece & Fiber Sourcebook: More Than 200 Fibers, from Animal to Spun Yarn.* North Adams, MA: Storey Publishing, 2011.

Elkins, Nathan. *A Monument to Dynasty and Death: The Story of Rome's Colosseum and the Emperors Who Built It.* Baltimore, MD: Johns Hopkins University Press, 2019.

Ensminger, M. E. *Sheep and Wool Science.* Danville, IL: The Interstate Printers & Publishers, 1970.

Gould, Francesca. *Why Fish Fart & Other Useless or Gross Information About the World.* New York: Jeremy P. Tarcher/Penguin, 2009.

Handwerk, Brian. "Feeling Overtaxed? The Romans Would Tax Your Urine." *National Geographic*, April 14, 2016.

Harvey, Brian K. *Daily Life in Ancient Rome: A Sourcebook.* Indianapolis, IN: Hackett Publishing Company, 2016.

Hill, Duncan. *Ancient Rome: From the Republic to the Empire.* Bath, UK: Parragon Books, 2010.

Jansen, Gemma C. M., Ann Olga Koloski-Ostrow, and Eric M. Moormann, eds. *Roman Toilets: Their Archaeology and Cultural History.* Leuven, Belgium: Peeters, 2011.

Jenkins, David, ed. *The Cambridge History of Western Textiles.* Cambridge, UK: Cambridge University Press, 2003.

Leon, Vicki. *Working IX to V: Orgy Planners, Funeral Clowns, and Other Prized Professions for the Ancient World.* New York: Walker and Company, 2007.

Moeller, Walter O. *The Wool Trade of Ancient Pompeii.* Netherlands: Leiden E. J. Brill, 1976.

Ray, Hannah, Daniella Saetta, and Treavor H. Boyer. "Characterization of Urea Hydrolysis in Fresh Human Urine and Inhibition by Chemical Addition." *Environmental Science: Water Research & Technology* 4 (2018): 87–98.

Robinson, Tony. *The Worst Jobs in History: Two Thousand Years of Miserable Employment.* London: Pan Books, 2004.

Smith, William, ed. *Dictionary of Greek and Roman Antiquities*, 3rd ed. London: William Clowes and Sons, Limited, 1890.

Chapter 10: A Cart o' Poop

Boxer, Sarah. "Threat to Archaeology: The Privy Digger." *New York Times*, July 28, 2001.

Breverton, Terry. *Everything You Ever Wanted to Know About the Tudors But Were Afraid to Ask*. Gloucestershire: Amberley Publishing, 2014.

Carter, W. Hodding. *Flushed: How the Plumber Saved Civilization*. New York: Atria Books, 2006.

Cartwright, Mark. "Medieval Hygiene." *World History Encyclopedia*. December 7, 2018. https://www.worldhistory.org/Medieval_Hygiene/.

Dyer, Christopher. *Making a Living in the Middle Ages: The People of Britain 850–1520*. New Haven, CT: Yale University Press, 2002.

Hart-Davis, Adam. *Thunder, Flush and Thomas Crapper: An Encyclopedia*. North Pomfret, VT: Trafalgar Square Publishing, 1997.

Newman, Paul. *Daily Life in the Middle Ages*. Jefferson, NC: McFarland & Company, 2001.

Sosna, Daniel, and Lenka Brunclíková, eds. *Archaeologies of Waste: Encounters with the Unwanted*. Oxford, UK: Oxbow Books, 2017.

Suffolk, Woodbridge. *Urban Bodies: Communal Health in the Late Medieval English Towns and Cities*. Boydell Press: Woodbridge, Suffolk, 2013.

World Bank Group. "Community-led total sanitation in rural areas: an approach that works." Water and Sanitation Program Washington, D.C. February 1, 2007. https://documents1.worldbank.org/curated/en/672891468324551045/pdf/396690Total0sanitation01PUBLIC1.pdf

Chapter 11: From Pelt to Belt

Blair, John and Nigel Ramsay, eds. *English Medieval Industries: Craftsmen, Techniques, Products*. London: The Hambledon Press, 1991.

Covington, Anthony D., and William R. Wise. *Tanning Chemistry: The Science of Leather*, 2nd ed. London: Royal Society of Chemistry, 2019.

Gies, Frances, and Joseph Gies. *Daily Life in Medieval Times: A Vivid, Detailed Account of Birth, Marriage and Death; Food, Clothing and Housing; Love and Labor in Europe of the Middle Ages.* New York: Black Dog & Leventhal Publishers, 1969, 1974, 1990.

Gould, Francesca. *Why Fish Fart & Other Useless or Gross Information About the World.* New York: Jeremy P. Tarcher/Penguin, 2009.

Kite, Marion, and Roy Thomson. *Conservation of Leather and Related Materials.* Oxford, UK: Butterworth-Heinemann, 2006.

Mayhew, Henry. *London Labour and the London Poor: The Classical Study of the Culture of Poverty and the Criminal Classes in the 19th Century.* New York: Dover Publications, Inc., 1968.

Petersen, Christine. *The Tanner.* Tarrytown, NY: Marshall Cavendish, 2012.

Reed, R. *Ancient Skins, Parchments and Leathers.* New York: Seminar Press, 1972.

Robinson, Tony. *The Worst Jobs in History: Two Thousand Years of Miserable Employment.* London: Pan Books, 2004.

Timeline History Channel. *The Worst Jobs in History—The Victorian Age.* Accessed November 29, 2022. https://www.youtube.com/watch?v=KaaZa-siRzgU.

Chapter 12: TP Holder for the King

Ackroyd, Peter. *Tudors: The History of England from Henry VIII to Elizabeth I.* New York: Thomas Dunne Books, 2012.

Belofsky, Nathan. *Strange Medicine: A Shocking History of Real Medical Practices Through the Ages.* New York: A Perigee Book, 2013.

Borman, Tracy. *The Private Lives of the Tudors.* New York: Grove Press, 2016.

Breverton, Terry. *Everything You Ever Wanted to Know About the Tudors But Were Afraid to Ask.* Gloucestershire: Amberley Publishing, 2014.

Chalmers, C. R., and E. J. Chaloner. "500 Years Later: Henry VIII, Leg Ulcers and the Course of History." *Journal of the Royal Society of Medicine* 102, no. 12 (2008): 514–17.

Gidlow, Christopher. *Life in a Tudor Palace.* Gloucestershire: Sutton Publishing, 2007.

Selected Bibliography

González-Crussí, Frank. *A Short History of Medicine*. New York: Modern Library, 2007.

Hart-Davis, Adam. *Thunder, Flush and Thomas Crapper: An Encyclopedia*. North Pomfret, VT: Trafalgar Square Publishing, 1997.

Hutchinson, Robert. *Young Henry: The Rise of Henry VIII*. New York: Thomas Dunne Books, 2011.

Matusiak, John. *Henry VIII: The Life and Rule of England's Nero*. Gloucestershire: The History Press, 2013.

Ray, C. Claiborne. "Marsupial Maintenance." *New York Times*, August 13, 2012.

Sim, Alison. *Masters & Servants in Tudor England*. Gloucestershire: The History Press, 2006.

"The Enema—Heir to the Clyster." *S.A. Medical Journal*, April 26, 1947.

Weir, Alison. *Henry VIII—The King and His Court*. New York: Ballantine Publishing Group, 2001.

Worsley, Lucy. *If Walls Could Talk: An Intimate History of the Home*. New York: Walker & Company, 2011.

Chapter 13: A Poo Explosion

Bown, Stephen R. *A Most Damnable Invention: Dynamite, Nitrates, and the Making of the Modern World*. New York: Thomas Dunne Books, 2005.

Chaline, Eric. *Fifty Minerals That Changed the Course of History*. Buffalo, NY: Firefly Books, 2012.

Cressy, David. *Saltpeter: The Mother of Gunpowder*. Oxford, UK: Oxford University Press, 2013.

Gould, Francesca. *Why Fish Fart & Other Useless or Gross Information About the World*. New York: Jeremy P. Tarcher/Penguin, 2009.

Irwin, Patrick G. J., Daniel Toledo, Ryan Garland, Nicholas A. Teanby, Leigh N. Fletcher, Glenn A. Orton, and Bruno Bézard. "Detection of Hydrogen Sulfide Above the Clouds in Uranus's Atmosphere." *Nature Astronomy* 2 (2018): 420–27.

Niermeier-Dohoney, Justin. "'Rusticall Chymistry': Alchemy, Saltpeter Projects, and Experimental Fertilizers in Seventeenth-Century English Agriculture." *History of Science*, September 17, 2021.

Schultz, Colin. "The Moon Smells Like Gunpowder." *Smithsonian Magazine*. August 27, 2014. https://www.smithsonianmag.com/smart-news/moon-smells-gunpowder-180952494/

Chapter 14: The Ultimate Treasure Hunt!

Ackroyd, Peter. *London Under: The Secret History Beneath the Streets*. New York: Nan A. Talese/Doubleday, 2011.

Black, Maggie, and Ben Fawcett. *The Last Taboo: Opening the Door on the Global Sanitation Crisis*. London: Earthscan, 2008.

Carter, W. Hodding. *Flushed: How the Plumber Saved Civilization*. New York: Atria Books, 2006.

Dash, Mike. "Quite Likely the Worst Job Ever." *Smithsonian Magazine*, June 29, 2012.

Eschner, Kat. "Friction Matches Were a Boon to Those Lighting Fires—Not So Much to Matchmakers." *Smithsonian Magazine*, November 27, 2017.

George, Rose. *The Big Necessity: The Unmentionable World of Human Waste and Why it Matters*. New York: Metropolitan Books, 2008.

Halliday, Stephen. *The Great Stink of London: Sir Joseph Bazalgette and the Cleansing of the Victorian Capital*. Gloucestershire: Sutton Publishing, 1999.

Jackson, Lee. *Dirty Old London: The Victorian Fight Against Filth*. New Haven, CT: Yale University Press, 2014.

Keyser, Amber. *Underneath It All: A History of Women's Underwear*. Minneapolis: Twenty-First Century Books, 2018.

Mayhew, Henry. *London Labour and the London Poor: The Classical Study of the Culture of Poverty and the Criminal Classes in the 19th Century*. New York: Dover Publications, Inc., 1968.

Oneill, Therese. *Unmentionable: The Victorian Lady's Guide to Sex, Marriage, and Manners*. New York: Little Brown and Company, 2016.

Picard, Liza. *Victorian London: The Life of a City 1840–1870*. New York: St. Martin's Press, 2005.

Westerhoff, Paul, Sungyun Lee, Yu Yang, Gwyneth W. Gordon, Kiril Hristovski, Rolf U. Halden, and Pierre Herckes. "Characterization, Recovery Opportunities, and Valuation of Metals in Municipal Sludges from U.S. Wastewater Treatment Plants Nationwide." *Environmental Science & Technology* 49, no. 16 (2015): 9479–88.

Chapter 15: The Bird Poop Blues

Bown, Stephen R. *A Most Damnable Invention: Dynamite, Nitrates, and the Making of the Modern World.* New York: Thomas Dunne Books, 2005.

Cushman, Gregory T. *Guano and the Opening of the Pacific World: A Global Ecological History.* New York: Cambridge University Press, 2013.

Hollett, David. *More Precious Than Gold: The Story of the Peruvian Guano Trade.* Madison, NJ: Fairleigh Dickinson University Press, 2008.

Johnston, Paul F. "The Smithsonian and the 19th Century Guano Trade: This Poop Is Crap." *Natural Museum of American History*, May 31, 2017.

Skaggs, Jimmy M. *The Great Guano Rush.* New York: St. Martin's Griffin, 1994.

Chapter 16: Born Unlucky

American Society of Civil Engineers. "2021 Infrastructure Report Card." 2022. https://www.infrastructurereportcard.org.

Department of Social Justice and Empowerment. Government of India. "Annual Report 2020–2021." 2021. https://socialjustice.gov.in/writereaddata /UploadFile/ANNUAL_REPORT_2021_ENG.pdf.

George, Rose. *The Big Necessity: The Unmentionable World of Human Waste and Why It Matters.* New York: Metropolitan Books, 2008.

Rao, Shashank. "Bio-Toilets on Trains to Keep Tracks Free of Yuck." *The Free Press Journal*, June 4, 2021.

Royal Collection Trust. "Buckingham Palace." https://www.rct.uk/sites/default /files/Buckingham_Palace_Fact_Sheet.pdf.

Safi, Michael. "'I'm Born to Do This': Condemned by Caste, India's Sewer Cleaners Risk Death Daily." *The Guardian*, March 3, 2019.

United Nations. "Groundwater and Sanitation—Making the Invisible Visible." 2022. https://www.un.org/en/observances/toilet-day.

United States Environmental Protection Agency. "Combined Sewer Overflow Basics." Last updated April 28, 2023. https://www.epa.gov/npdes /combined-sewer-overflow-basics.

Varma, Aishwarya. "'No Death' Due to Manual Scavenging? A Tragic Truth Buried in 'Technicalities.'" *The Quint*, July 30, 2020.

World Health Organization. "Drinking-water." March 2022. https://www.who.int/news-room/fact-sheets/detail/drinking-water.

World Health Organization. "Who Cares About Toilets?" November 2021. https://www.who.int/europe/news/item/19-11-2021-who-cares-about-toilets.

A SPEWING OF THANKS

Writing *Waist-Deep in Dung* definitely involved doing some pretty stomach-churning research, but in all other ways the job was relatively tame. I didn't need to stomp in any vats of stale pee, pluck any wiggling maggots out of dead bodies, or mop up any revolting puke piles. And not only was the act of writing this book a rather palatable one, but at every step of the way I received help from so, so many others.

There is my agent, Jim McCarthy, who is the very best advocate and ally I could have asked for. I thank my lucky stars every day that he is my agent!

There are the editors who shepherded this book through each step of the process . . . from Julia Sooy, who first saw the potential in this book; to Rachel Murray; to Kortney Nash, who finished things off with an absolute bang.

There are Julia Bianchi, Alexei Esikoff, Jie Yang, and the rest of the incredible crew at Godwin Books, Henry Holt Books for Young Readers, and Macmillan Children's Publishing

Group who somehow, incredibly, made this publishing dream of mine a reality.

There is Korwin Briggs, who once again brought my text to life with his h-i-l-a-r-i-o-u-s illustrations. Korwin—you are an Absolute Genius!

There are my critique partners—Sarah Martyn Crowell, Cynthia Manocchia, Val McCammon, Christopher Millay, Victor Suthammanont, and Annie Vihtelic—who have been utterly invaluable as friends and as writing buddies. I would 1000% trudge through a sewer for any one of you!

There are Kai and Myrtle and the rest of the Lakeside squad. Thank you for the accountability, the comradery, and of course, the laughs!

There is Mark Cullen, research librarian at the Verona Public Library. Without him, my stomach-churning research would have been waaaay more unpleasant!

And last but certainly not least, there is my family. I have to give a huge thank-you to my amazing parents, brother, and sister who have always been there for me, no matter what. And to my daughters, Sam and Rachel, for once again enduring the embarrassment of having a mom who writes about poop. And of course, I've saved a million and one thank-yous for my husband, without whose unwavering support I might never have had the guts to hit Send on my very first query letter. Thank you for giving me wings!

GLOSSARY

A

Alchemy: a medieval science in which one attempts to turn a base metal (such as lead or copper) into gold, an elixir of life (aka the ticket to living f-o-r-e-v-e-r), and a cure for all diseases.

Ammonia: a colorless, toxic, and (extraordinarily) stinky gas that dissolves easily in water. It is commonly used in explosives, fertilizers, and cleaning products.

Anatomy: a branch of science that deals with the identification and description of the structures that make up living things.

Anesthetic: a drug that makes a body less able to feel pain.

Anticoagulant: a substance that keeps a person's blood from clumping together and forming clots.

Apothecary: a person who prepares and dispenses medications (like a pharmacist) and a place where medications are sold (like a pharmacy).

Asphyxiation: a shortage of oxygen in the body that can cause an individual to pass out. Or die!

B

Barber-surgeon: a barber who also performed surgeries and dentistry. Their list of services might have included cutting hair, bloodletting, chopping off limbs, trimming beards, and yanking out rotten teeth.

Bedpan: a shallow container used to collect urine and feces from a person who can't get out of bed.

Bloodletting: the withdrawal of blood from a person's body for medical reasons, such as to treat seizures, gout, or sore throats. (Spoiler alert: it didn't *actually* treat any of these things.)

C

Cadaver: a dead body, especially a dead *human* body meant to be dissected.

Caste system: a social structure in which people are divided into different groups, or castes. The caste an individual is born into will determine who they can marry, what jobs they can do, etc.

Cataract: a medical condition in which a part of the eye (called the *lens*) becomes cloudy. Because the lens is supposed to be easy to see through, a cataract makes a person's vision blurry or hazy.

Cesspit: a hole in the ground meant to collect and store human waste. (Basically . . . it's a giant poo pit.)

Chamber pot: a bowl-like container that serves as a portable toilet. A chamber pot is typically stored in a "chamber" (which is a fancy word for a private room, especially a bedroom).

Close stool: a portable toilet shaped like a box or stool with an opening on top. Anything plopping or dribbling through the hole will wind up in the chamber pot concealed within the structure.

Constipation: when you don't poop frequently enough and your poop gets all dry and hard.

Contaminate: to make something dirty, harmful, or even poisonous by introducing a polluting substance.

Corpse: a dead body.

Cremation: when a dead body is disposed of by burning it to ashes.

D

Decomposition: the process of decaying . . . or rotting away.

Dissection: the act of cutting something open—like a dead person, an animal, or a plant—to study what's inside.

E

Embalmer: a person who treats dead bodies so as to prevent them from decaying (or rotting away).

Glossary

Enema: the injection of a liquid up someone's rear end, most often done to help a constipated person poo.

Entomology: the scientific study of insects. (Even the really icky ones like cockroaches and bedbugs and earwigs.)

Enzyme: a protein that speeds up a chemical reaction, such as *pepsin*— an enzyme in your stomach that helps break down the food you eat.

F

Fertilizer: a substance, such as animal poop or a mixture of chemicals, that can be added to soil to help plants grow.

Forensic entomology: a field of study that uses insects (especially the insects found on dead bodies) to solve crimes.

Forensics: using scientific knowledge to solve crimes.

Fuller: a person who cleaned and thickened cloth (often with the help of some good old-fashioned urine).

Fuller's earth: a clay that's great at absorbing grease and oil.

G

Garderobe: a medieval toilet, especially in a castle.

Gongfermor: a person who removed human waste from cesspits and privies. Also called gong farmers, gong scourers, and night soil men.

Guano: the excrement (i.e., dung) of bats and seabirds.

I

Indiana Jones: the main character in a series of movies. The ancient-artifact-finding archaeologist is well-known for his bullwhip, fedora hat, and ophidiophobia (fear of snakes).

L

Leech: a segmented worm that has a sucker on both ends. Most leech species are parasites that feed on the blood of other animals.

Life cycle: the series of developmental stages an organism goes through during its lifetime (such as a butterfly going from egg to caterpillar to chrysalis to butterfly).

M

Maggot: the squishy-bodied, legless larva of a fly. (Maggots are also exceedingly disgusting, but my editor doesn't want me putting that in the "official" definition . . . so *shhhh.*)

Manual scavenger: a person who removes human waste from sewers, septic systems, or dry latrines, all by hand.

Middle Ages: a time period commonly defined as falling between the collapse of the Roman Empire in the fifth century and the start of the Renaissance. It is also called the medieval period.

Mudlark: a person who searched for valuable objects in river mud, especially the mud along the River Thames in London.

Mummify: to turn into a mummy, as with a dead body.

N

Natron: a mineral salt found naturally in certain salty lakes, including some lakes in Egypt.

Nitrate: a compound containing nitrogen and oxygen. Nitrates are commonly found in fertilizers and explosives.

O

Opium: a highly addictive drug made from a flowering plant called the opium poppy. Opium reduces pain, causes sleepiness, and—if taken at the wrong dose—can KILL a person.

P

Potassium nitrate: *see Saltpeter.*

R

Renaissance: a period of European history that marked the transition from the Middle Ages to modern times. It lasted *approximately* from the fourteenth to seventeenth centuries.

Resurrection men: men who dug up recently buried bodies and sold them. Also called resurrectionists, body snatchers, and sack-'em-up men.

S

Saltpeter: a white substance (with a sharp, salty taste) used to help preserve meats, as a fertilizer, and as an ingredient in gunpowder. Its chemical name is potassium nitrate.

Saltpeter man: a man who procured saltpeter so it could be used to make gunpowder.

Sanitize: to clean or disinfect.

T

Tanner: a person who turns animal skins into leather.

Toadstool: a fungus that typically has an umbrella-like cap situated upon a stalk. (Kind of like a mushroom, aka *the grossest food ever.*)

Tosher: a person who looked for treasure in the sewers, especially the sewers of London during the Victorian era.

Trepanning: a surgical procedure in which a hole is made in a person's SKULL!

U

Ulcer: an open sore that *really* doesn't want to heal. Ulcers can be found on the skin (like Henry VIII's reeking leg ulcers) or somewhere you can't see (like your stepdad's stomach ulcer).

Urea: a waste product found in mammal pee. It is formed as the result of protein breakdown.

V

Victorian era: a time period in British history most commonly defined as lasting from 1837–1901 (the years Queen Victoria sat upon the throne).

VIP: a Very Important Person. Like Abraham Lincoln, or Sir Isaac Newton, or the person who makes guacamole at Chipotle.

W

Waiting mortuary: a facility where newly dead bodies were kept and observed until they clearly began to rot. Its purpose: to prevent a person from being buried if they were, in fact, still alive.

Wastewater: water that has already been used, such as bathwater, water flushed down a toilet, or water used by a factory. Wastewater is often contaminated with bacteria, chemicals, human waste, etc.

Workhouse: a building in Britain where the very poor could work in exchange for food and housing.

Index

Index

207

M

N

O

P

Q

R

S